An examination of the earliest period of Russian history for which written sources survive. Mrs Chadwick examines Russia's own rich historical traditions and chronicles, and assesses the extent of oral elements. She relates to these, Greek, Oriental and Scandinavian writings. She isolates the various traditions within the Russian chronicles. Her work is basic to any study of the history of Russia.

THE
BEGINNINGS OF RUSSIAN HISTORY:

AN ENQUIRY INTO SOURCES

Early Christian Church excavated in the Rock at Inkerman in the Crimea

from the painting by C. Bussoli, *The Beautiful Scenery...throughout the Crimea*, Plate 10

The Beginnings of

RUSSIAN HISTORY:
AN ENQUIRY INTO SOURCES

BY

N. K. CHADWICK
Fellow of Newnham College, Cambridge

CAMBRIDGE
AT THE UNIVERSITY PRESS
1946
REPRINTED
1966

PUBLISHED BY

THE SYNDICS OF THE CAMBRIDGE UNIVERSITY PRESS

Bentley House, 200 Euston Road, London, N.W.1
American Branch: 32 East 57th Street, New York, N.Y. 10022
West African Office: P.M.B. 5181, Ibadan, Nigeria

Publisher's Note

Cambridge University Press Library Editions are reissues of out-of-print
standard works from the Cambridge catalogue. The texts are unrevised
and, apart from minor corrections, reproduce the latest published edition.

First published 1946
Reprinted 1966

First printed in Great Britain at the University Press, Cambridge
Library of Congress Catalogue Card Number 46–6223
Reprinted in the United States of America

To

JOAN PERNEL STRACHEY,

MY FORMER TUTOR AND PRINCIPAL,

I dedicate this small volume
In admiration and
affection.

107749

Coacervavi omne quod inveni...quod multi doctores atque librarii scribere temptaverunt, nescio quo pacto difficilius reliquerunt, an propter mortalitates frequentissimas vel clades creberrimas bellorum. Rogo ut omnis lector qui legerit hunc librum det veniam mihi, qui ausus sum post tantos tanta scribere, quasi garrula avis vel quasi quidam invalidus arbiter. Cedo illi qui plus noverit in ista peritia satis quam ego. Explicit apologia.

NENNIUS.

CONTENTS

PREFACE

This little book is an attempt to present a clearer picture of Russia in the earliest period for which we have records. The country is especially rich in historical traditions relating to the earliest period of her history. She is also fortunate in the possession of a chronicle composed early in the twelfth century, and carrying back the records of events in the valley of the Dnêpr to the Viking Age, and even earlier. It has long been recognised that much of the material incorporated in the earliest annals of the earliest Russian chronicle is derived from oral tradition; but whether from poetry or saga, whether from Russian or Scandinavian sources, has never been determined. My first task has been to seek to ascertain with more precision the nature and extent of some of the oral elements, both Scandinavian and Russian, which have been utilised by the compiler.

During the last twenty years much new material bearing on early Russian history has come to light from the written records of the countries on the periphery of Russia. This has been found chiefly in Greek and Arabic writings; but something can be gleaned also from references in Persian and Armenian and other Oriental records. The important bearing of Scandinavian historical tradition is coming to be more fully recognised. My second task has been to make a beginning in the interpretation of early Russian historical records in the light of such external evidence from peripheral countries.

Finally, I have attempted to bring the entries in the Russian chronicle into relationship with one another, with a view to determining the relevance of widely separated events and campaigns for the development and fluctuations of policy, and the growth of the state. Perhaps the most important element in this task has been to determine the personal sympathies and preoccupations of the compiler, and the bias necessarily reflected in such records. These considerations naturally lead to suggestions

as to the milieu in which the records have been made, even under
what auspices they have originated, and what purpose they were
originally intended to serve.

My work has convinced me that the part played by the
Scandinavians in Russian history has not been clearly understood.
The Scandinavians in Russia, as in the West, were in no sense
originators of the state, but an important episode in its history.
By their military skill and organisation into standing garrisons,
they enabled the more advanced Russians, who had long been
under Greek influence, to maintain themselves against waves of
aggression from the steppe. The Greeks lent support to the
Russians as a valuable buffer state between themselves and the
Scandinavians. Russian internal and external policy was guided
throughout by the necessity of maintaining conditions which
rendered agriculture possible, and also by the necessity of
acquiring money whereby to purchase immunity from the
pillaging nomads whose depredations threatened to starve them,
and to pay their 'Varangian' mercenaries to support them by
arms. The scope of this brief study, published under war-time
conditions, and with regrettably few of the relevant books
available, does not permit of a detailed treatment, and my work
is of necessity suggestive rather than exhaustive. I have thought
it worth while to publish it even in this brief form in the hope
that in the future a fuller study of early Russian history will be
made on the lines which I have suggested by scholars more
competent to deal with the wealth of relevant material.

My thanks are due first of all to Newnham College for
awarding me the Sarah Smithson Research Fellowship, during
a part of the tenure of which this work was done. The gracious
kindness and friendliness of the Principal and Fellows have been
a constant help and stimulus to my work during the difficult war
years. I have also been fortunate in the help which I have received from a number of scholars. In particular I am grateful
to Professor Sir Ellis Minns, who read the work in manuscript and
made a number of corrections and suggestions in regard to matters
Russian, and who also lent me books. Professor Minorsky has

read through the proofs and made many helpful suggestions. I am further indebted to His Excellency S. H. Taqizadeh, the Iranian Ambassador, for some important references to Oriental sources; to Professor Bailey for Armenian material, and for the Armenian translation incorporated in the text; to Miss Mary Beare, to Professor Donald Robertson and to Professor D. W. Thomas for allowing me to consult them on several questions; and to my husband for help in the reading of the proofs. They have most generously placed their learning at my disposal, and I alone am responsible for such shortcomings as remain. For some of these I may perhaps plead in extenuation the almost prohibitive difficulties under which the work has been carried on. The scope of my book and, indeed, of my own studies, has been extending eastwards, even while my book was going through the Press, and I want to thank the Syndics and the staff for their indulgence and patience with my many additions and corrections in proof, as well as for producing the book. I am especially indebted to Miss Hennings, who has made the Index.

The extract contained in Appendix I is from the *Tadjārib al-Umam* by Ibn Miskawaih, translated from the Arabic by the late Professor D. S. Margoliouth.

N. K. CHADWICK

NEWNHAM COLLEGE
CAMBRIDGE
1945

CHAPTER I

THE EARLY RECORDS

The fascination of Russian studies relating to the early period of the national life lies largely in the fact that the records are in a state of transition between legend and history. They are quite different in character from the early historical writings of Scandinavian lands, where annalistic history, with its exact chronology, is unknown. On the other hand they differ essentially from our own Anglo-Saxon Chronicle, in which the element of saga is reduced to a minimum, and of which the annals appear to be virtually independent of panegyric or heroic poetry. The earliest Russian records have made use of practically every form of historical source—saga and heroic poetry, biography, annals, the reports of eyewitnesses, legal documents, such as international treaties, even the written records of books. All these sources of information have been utilised by the compiler; and surely no chronicler ever showed himself more liberal and more imaginative in the best sense of the word in the collection of his materials, or more skilled and constructive in his use of them to build up a vivid and readable, and, in general, dignified and convincing picture of a nation's history.

The earliest Russian historical records are embodied in a written chronicle, composed, like most medieval historical works, in monastic circles. It was almost certainly written in a monastery in Kiev, whether as a single or a composite work. Its form is roughly annalistic. This annalistic form is derived ultimately from the Eusebian tables; but the more immediate form of the chronicle was doubtless directly suggested by other similar chronicles composed during the Dark and the Middle Ages on contemporary Greek and Latin models. The individuality of the Russian chronicle lies in the freedom with which the compiler intersperses his laconic entries with extended and vivid narratives, often amounting to complete short stories on historical subjects, and at times showing clearly that they are derived from ambitious oral narratives of a highly elaborate and artistic nature. Such entries are made under the years to which they are relevant, so that the annalistic form is still retained, though utilised as the merest skeleton, and enriched with every kind of matter which the compiler could find bearing upon his subject, not excluding lengthy quotations from the scriptures and hagiological writings.

The history of Russia for the earliest period, therefore, resolves itself inevitably into a study of sources. And, moreover, so far as written sources are concerned, it confines itself largely to a history of the valley of the Dnêpr, and more especially of the city state of Kiev—of Kiev, and, in a lesser degree, of Novgorod. This natural preoccupation of the chronicler with his own area has given rise to a widespread assumption that the history of Russia begins in, and was for long confined to, the western part of the country. It is now known, however, that the history of civilisation in Russia began long before the earliest period for which we have records, and that the eastern waterways were developed at least as early, if not earlier than the valley of the Dnêpr. For further knowledge of the early history of eastern Russia we await the results of archaeological and Oriental re- searches. For the west we are fortunate in the possession of comparatively early Russian written sources of information.

The history of Kiev in early times, as we see it in the pages of the earliest chronicle, falls naturally into some five periods. This is not an artificial classification, though it does not necessarily correspond to actual changes or phases in the history of the period. It lies in the nature of the records.

1. First of all we have a period known to us chiefly through antiquarian speculation based apparently on faint traditions of the ancient mercantile importance of pre-Norse Kiev.

2. Next comes the traditional account of the establishment of Scandinavian power, beginning with Rurik, and developing into a long and detailed saga of Oleg, the first ruler of Kiev of whom we have circumstantial knowledge, and of his fosterage of

Rurik's son Igor, and of the reigns of Igor, his wife Olga, and his son Svyatoslav.

3. The life of Vladimir, who is generally regarded as the true founder of the Russian state and of the Russian Church. How far this view is in accordance with the evidence, we shall see better as we proceed. The account of his reign is derived partly from saga, partly from a written life of the saint, which may have already incorporated the saga material before it came into the hands of the chronicler. It is very possible that other early writings of Greek or Khazar provenance were also available for this period.

4. For the reigns of Yaroslav and Svyatopolk, Vladimir's immediate successors, it is evident that the chronicler had at his disposal a wealth of evidence in the form of saga, and panegyric, perhaps also of elegiac poetry. This was probably partly in the Russian, but almost certainly also largely in the Norse language.

5. For the period of the time of Vladimir II, Monomakh, in whose reign the chronicle as we have it was probably compiled, the writer has made use of the reports of eyewitnesses, and of hearsay; of local events and local political opinion and movements in and near Kiev itself; of family history in the form of family saga. He has threaded his way through a maze of conflicting reports, and biased views, and clashing interests in one of the most difficult periods of the nation's history. Inevitably the bias of the historian makes itself especially felt in his own day, and a critical scrutiny of the pages of the chronicle becomes particularly necessary in judging, not so much what actually happened, as why the events took place.

It will be apparent at a glance that the materials of which the earliest Russian chronicle is composed are of very uneven historical value. Before we can hope to begin the study of the actual history of Russia in the early period we must first make a critical survey of our sources. To do this an intensive study of the text is required. It is not enough to make a critical examination of the probable historical value of each annal, or group of annals. It ought to be possible, by bringing the information of different annals together, to reconstruct, in some measure, the life of the times at which they hint. It is necessary to study the bearing of one annal upon another and the significance of the juxtaposition of certain annals, and of certain events, even when these are recounted with a semblance of independence; to trace the operation of cause and effect where the annalist may have failed to do so. Moreover, it is not enough to study Kiev in isolation. While following the course of events here, it is necessary to have in view what is happening in the north, and to watch the bearing and the repercussions of the quarrels and alliances, the invasions and expeditions of other states, on that of Kiev; to realise the correlation of events in the Russian microcosm.

Finally it is important to supplement our direct knowledge of Russian history from the contemporary records of the surrounding peoples. Illumination must and will come from Greek educated historians of the period, as well as from Arabic and other Oriental sources; perhaps from fragmentary documents of the Khazars; from medieval Latin writers who were in touch with the western parts of the Slavonic area. Above all it will come from the vast wealth of Norse literature, which is still virtually an unexploited gold mine for Russian history and literature. A few isolated studies have already appeared, showing that the relevance of Norse studies in this field is coming to be realised; but as yet very little has been achieved by scholars fully qualified to work at the Norse background of the Viking Age in Russia, and in general little has been done beyond the sporadic indication of chance similarities in the two literatures. A fuller study of the interrelation of the two cultures by scholars equally well qualified to handle both the Norse and the Russian material, and with a knowledge of contemporary Oriental and Greek records, is urgently needed. In the following pages it has not been possible for me to do more than to indicate some of the lines which it seems to me such an investigation ought to take, and the channels of information which may profitably be pursued. I have only ventured to do so in the hope that someone better qualified than myself will carry the study further along such lines.

The earliest native Russian document which gives direct information relating to Kiev is the *Povêst Vremennykh Lêt*, 'The Chronicle of Contemporary Years'.[1] The earliest form of the text is preserved in two important versions, known as the Laurentian and the Hypatian.[2] This work has been traditionally ascribed to one Nestor, a monk in the Pechersk monastery at Kiev (c. 1056–1114); but a comparison of the contents of the chronicle with works indubitably by Nestor has demonstrated the fact that he cannot have been the author of the former.[3] Many scholars hold that the chronicle has incorporated earlier annals, and that the final compilation was the work of Sylvester, Abbot of St Michael's monastery of Kiev.[4] All that can be said with certainty is that the work was probably composed, or at least assumed its present form, about the year 1113.[5]

In the year A.M. 6624 (A.D. 1116), we read the following entry in the Laurentian text: 'In the hope of God's grace, I, Sylvester, abbot of St Michael's, wrote these books of the Annals, hoping to receive mercy from God, in the time of Prince Volodimer, prince of Kiev, and of my own abbacy of St Michael's in the year 6624 (1116). May whosoever reads this book remember me in his prayers.'

It is extremely probable, as Cross observes, that some method of recording historical events had been employed in Kiev from

[1] The only form of the text of the *Povêst* which has been accessible to me is the *Chronica Nestoris* (*Textus Russico-Slovenicus*), ed. by Fr. Miklosich (Vindobona, 1860). This text is in Old Slavonic, and for the convenience of English readers I have given my references where possible to the English translation by Samuel H. Cross, *The Russian Primary Chronicle* (Cambridge, Mass. 1930).

[2] The Laurentian text was named from the copyist who prepared it at Suzdal in 1377. The Hypatian dates from the middle of the fifteenth century, and was probably copied at Pskov from a south Russian original, but named from the monastery of Kostroma in which it was discovered. See Cross, *op. cit.* p. 78.   [3] See Cross, *op. cit.* pp. 80 ff.

[4] See Michell, Forbes and Beazley, *The Chronicle of Novgorod* (London, 1914), p. xxxvii; cf. also Klyuchevski, *History of Russia* (transl. by C. J. Hogarth, London, 1911), Vol. I, pp. 13 ff.

[5] Cross, *op. cit.* p. 97.

the period of the introduction of Christianity and of Greek culture under Vladimir I, and that these records would be utilised in the compilation of the *Povêst*. But in general it would seem natural to take Sylvester's statement as a simple expression of fact, and to conclude that the *Povêst* was compiled in its present form in the second decade of the twelfth century.

At the same time I cannot refrain from suggesting in this connection that sources of information other than Greek writings and Scandinavian oral tradition may have been accessible to the compiler or his predecessors. We shall see as we proceed that there is serious ground for believing that Jewish writings relating to the Khazars contain information relating to the rulers of Kiev in the early tenth century. Information such as this may have been accessible in Kiev, either directly from Khazar sources, or through some intermediary, such as the Greek churches on the shores of the Black Sea (cf. p. 45 below). The utilisation of Khazar sources of information by the Russians would be a simple matter after the capture of Sarkel (Bela Vezha) by Svyatoslav in 965. We have some evidence that the Khazars had books and libraries which they housed in the rock-cut churches, and that they were in the habit of referring to these as authorities on matters of the past (cf. p. 46 below). I am the more inclined to suggest that the possibility of Khazar records as one of the sources of the *Povêst* has been underestimated, in view of the fact that the mission of the various religions, notably Islamic, Greek and Jewish, to Vladimir I in an attempt to convert him, as we find this in the pages of the *Povêst*, finds an exact, even a verbal, parallel in a Khazar document to be referred to later.

The *Povêst* covers, roughly speaking, the period from the middle of the ninth to the second decade of the twelfth century, and it is to this period, and more especially to the earlier portion, that the heroic traditions are ascribed by the annalist.[1] In the traditional oral poetical narratives, known as *byliny*, these heroic

---

[1] For a brief discussion of the heroic conditions which prevailed in Kiev and other city states of western Russia during the Tatar invasions, see Chadwick, *Growth of Literature*, Vol. II (Cambridge, 1936), p. 24.

traditions are centred in Prince Vladimir of Kiev—whether Vladimir I (980–1015) or Vladimir II (1113–1125); but in the *Povêst* they are by no means confined to either of these two princes. The majority are assigned to the period which preceded the reign of Vladimir I; but they seem to have flourished at Kiev down to a much later date, as we see from many entries in the *Povêst* itself, notably the story of the encounter between the Kasog chief Rededya and Mstislav of Tmutorakan, s.a. 6530 (A.D. 1022); cf. p. 66 below. In actual fact the annals of the reign of Vladimir I are comparatively bare of heroic incidents. The annalist is concerned rather to show the importance of the events which led to the adoption of Christianity in 988, and to Vladimir's marriage with a Greek princess, and the consequent adoption of foreign culture at the court of Kiev.

The annals for the reign of Vladimir I and for the period which preceded are based partly on ecclesiastical (Greek) sources,[1] partly on diplomatic and other documents,[2] and partly on oral traditions.[3] The account, for example, of almost the whole of the so-called Scandinavian period is undoubtedly based on oral traditions.[4] Oral tradition is also responsible for the account of the conversion of the people of Kiev under Vladimir I; and of the part played by his uncle Dobrynya—whether these have come down wholly through the medium of such tradition, or through the intermediary form of a life of the saint.[5] On the other hand, there can be no reasonable doubt that from about A.D. 1050 to 1113 the information is derived from the accounts of eyewitnesses. In general, therefore, the information within this latter period, which includes the reign of Vladimir Monomakh, grandson of Yaroslav the Wise,[6] and great-grandson of Vladimir I, may be regarded as reliable in essentials in regard to actual matters of fact, such as the

[1] Cross, *op. cit.* p. 99.   [2] *Ib.* p. 103.   [3] *Ib.* p. 105.

[4] An early life of Olga is believed to have existed in written form, and this has no doubt yielded some material to the chronicler. Cf. p. 31 below.

[5] Cross, *op. cit.* p. 108.

[6] For the Norse and Russian evidence relating to the marriages of Yaroslav and his sons, see Cross, 'Yaroslav the Wise in Norse Tradition' *Speculum*, Vol. IV (1929), pp. 181 ff.

statement that Dobrynya was *voevoda* ('military commander') of Kiev under Mstislav Vladimirovich, and that he took part as such in the northern campaign of 1096.

The literary perspective of the chronicle, therefore, may be said to focus naturally on the events in Kiev which lead up to the reign of Monomakh; and the domestic and political relations of the princes and their wars which precede this are calculated to show both the importance of family unity in the face of the common enemy—the nomad menace; and the predominant element of Slavonic blood in the royal house of Kiev. In the preceding period the nationalistic aim of the chronicler is equally prominent. In particular we may point to the accounts of the careers of Svyatopolk and Yaroslav the Wise. The former, who depended for his support on the Pechenegs and Poles, is brought to ruin and a tragic end. Yaroslav himself, in so far as he depended on his Varangians, was repeatedly defeated and forced to flee. He is even represented as proposing to abandon his people and take refuge in Scandinavia; but the native population prevent him, and force him to fight the enemy. It is the native elements, the people themselves, the inhabitants of Kiev and Novgorod, and of the surrounding country, who rally around Yaroslav, and force him to fight the foreign invaders till a successful issue is reached. The course of these events will become clearer as we proceed.

The high light which is focused on the earliest period, and which culminates in the reign of Vladimir I, is carefully calculated to minimise the permanence of the Scandinavian element in the early history of the royal house and of the city state of Kiev. The whole Scandinavian rule is treated as a preface to the reign of Vladimir I, who is appropriately represented as a saint and founder of the Russian Church, and as the founder of the Russian (i.e. emphatically the Slavonic) kingdom of Kiev. It is with the intention of exalting these all-important features of Vladimir's life that the chronicler takes pains to assure us that his mother was Slavonic, and that he even Slavicises his name, which is in reality a Gothic (*Valdimir*) or a Scandinavian name

(*Valdimarr*). And it is obviously with this same end in view that he recounts at length the story of Vladimir's idols and his heathen activities in Kiev itself in early life, and those of his uncle Dobrynya, the *voevoda*, in Novgorod. By thus exalting Vladimir I as the first Slavonic ruler, the first founder of the Russian state, and the father of the Russian Church, the author of the *Povêst* has utilised the oral traditions of the Scandinavian period and the ecclesiastical records of the reign of Vladimir I to forward his aim of indicating how the entire course of Russian history has led up to a desired consummation in the rule of Monomakh, who is thus represented as partly Slavonic in descent, and exclusively nationalistic in outlook.

As Vasiliev points out,[1] Oleg, Igor and Svyatoslav were all in a position to make treaties with the Greeks; but under Vladimir matters changed, and a careful reading of his relations, and of those of his successors, with the Greeks suggests very strongly that Kiev had now declined to the position of some kind of vassal state to Byzantium. As a matter of fact, a careful reading of the *Povêst* itself makes it clear that the traditional founder of the state of Kiev as we know it, that is to say, of historical Kiev, was not Vladimir I, but Oleg. It is very possible that something of a nationalistic revival may have taken place as early as the reign of Vladimir I, carefully engineered by such *voevody* as Dobrynya and Blud, and that much was made of this in later times, both by the Church, and by the nationalistic elements so prominent under Yaroslav and under his grandson Svyatopolk, and finally under Vladimir II. But the traditions carefully recorded in the *Povêst* of Oleg's capture and occupation of Kiev— not from a primitive Slav population, but from a settled Norse community; of his subsequent foreign campaigns and victories; his successful raid on Tsargrad (Byzantium)—for whatever this is worth; and his treaty with the Greeks—again for what it is worth; all these make it clear that, in the opinion of the chronicler at least, Oleg was a ruler to whom tradition ascribed a paramount

[1] For the evidence, see his interesting article, 'Was Old Russia a Vassal State of Byzantium?' *Speculum*, Vol. VII (1932), pp. 350 ff.

place in the early history of Kiev. The chronicler himself has sought to minimise this importance. He tells us, for example, nothing of his origin or parentage, though he mentions that he was of Rurik's kin, and thus came to hold such a distinguished position among the Scandinavians themselves as is implied by his part as 'fosterer' to Rurik's son Igor.[1] In all probability Oleg was himself of the highest rank, and father to Olga, Igor's wife; but the chronicler is silent on the subject.

Yet there can be no doubt that the chronicler was himself aware of traditions which represented Oleg as of paramount importance in the early history of Kiev. Nothing shows this more clearly than his insertion of the text of a treaty which he claims to have been made between Oleg and the Greeks as the result of a successful raid by Oleg and his Varangian *druzhina* against Byzantium. It is stated in the *Povêst* that in this expedition in 907 Oleg and his ships appeared under the walls of the Greek capital, and after pillaging the suburbs, and killing many of the people, forced the Greek emperor, Leo VI, 'The Wise', to form a treaty with him. Neither Byzantine nor western sources mention such an expedition, or even Oleg's name; but Vasiliev points out[2] that the Greek history of Leo the Deacon,[3] which is an important authority for this period, puts into the mouth of John Tzimisces a threat to Svyatoslav which seems to have reference to this treaty: 'I hope you have not forgotten the defeat of your father Igor (Ἴγγορ), who, *having scorned the sworn agreements* (τὰς ἐνόρκους σπονδάς) came by sea to the imperial city with a great army and numerous vessels.' These 'sworn agreements' made with the Byzantine empire before Igor's time may, in Vasiliev's

[1] In the words of the *Povêst*: 'When Rurik had died (*sic*) he entrusted his realm to Oleg, because he was of his kindred, and he gave to him his young son Igor to rear, for he was very young' (Umershyu Ryurikovi predast knyazhenye svoye Olgovi, ot roda yemu sushchu, vdav yemu syn svoy na rutsê, Igorya, bê bo dêtesk velmi), *Povêst*, s.a. 6378–6387 (A.D. 870–879).

[2] *History of the Byzantine Empire*, Vol. I (Madison, 1928), p. 389; *Histoire de l'Empire Byzantin*, Vol. I (Paris, 1932), pp. 424 f.

[3] *Historiae*, VI, 10 (ed. Bonn), p. 106.

opinion, have been the agreement of Oleg reported in full by the Russian chronicler.

It has been suggested,[1] mainly on the grounds of internal evidence, that the text of Oleg's treaty, as given in the *Povêst*, is a fabrication. The main contention of the sceptics is that this text bears obvious traces of having been composed on the model of the later treaties of Igor and Svyatoslav, and of containing only such matter as could have been deduced from information drawn from the narrative of the *Povêst* itself. The validity of the treaty, together with those of Igor and Svyatoslav, is, however, accepted by most historians, including Vasiliev,[2] whose opinion should carry special weight in view of his expert knowledge of contemporary Greek history.

I cannot refrain from pointing out, however, that an examination of the proper names, mostly Scandinavian, appended to the treaty of Oleg, raises some rather serious questions. These names are not only unaccompanied by any epithets or honorifics, or other means of closer identification, such as are appended to the names at the. conclusion of the treaty of Igor with the Greeks, but they are themselves a totally different series of names from the latter. Moreover, the names themselves are quite unconvincing as signatures to a legal document. While the names which follow the treaty of Igor are the current names of the Viking Age, and look quite genuine, a high proportion of those appended to the treaty of Oleg are almost confined elsewhere to heroic tradition. If, as is possible, they were drawn from such a source, that is to say, if they are derived from heroic poetry current in Kiev at the time when the first written records were made, this fact is in itself interesting, as indicating the extent to which Scandinavian heroic poetry was current in Kiev at the time when the *Povêst* was composed. This evidence might, on further investigation, serve in some measure to reveal what particular traditions were current in Kiev at this period.

[1] See Mansikka, *Die Religion der Ostslaven* (Helsinki, 1922), pp. 30ff.
[2] See his *History of the Byzantine Empire, loc. cit.*; also his article in *Speculum*, Vol. VII (1932), p. 350.

It may indeed be questioned whether too much has not been made in modern times of the exclusive proprietary rights of the Norsemen in the foundation of the Russian kingdom, and of Russian civilisation and culture generally.[1] Of the solid contribution of the Norsemen to certain aspects of Russian national life there can be no doubt whatever. This has been demonstrated once for all by Thomsen,[2] and must be accepted as proved; but it is by no means the whole of the picture, though it is generally assumed to be the whole, partly because such a picture gains some support from archaeological evidence, partly because it is supported also by negative evidence. We have no written records of what existed in Russia before the Norsemen came. But it must be remembered that the Norsemen are rarely, if ever, found in the west to have made permanent settlements in what were merely 'promising sites', but always in centres which were already flourishing, and in rich settlements or towns, and we have no grounds for supposing that their procedure in the east would have been any different in this respect. Indeed the contrary may, I think, be assumed. On the other hand it must be remembered that archaeology is not very likely to afford evidence of rich settlements unless these had been fortified with wood or stone. Mere possible habitation sites, however rich, are not very likely to attract the attention of the excavator; but it must not be assumed that evidence of Norse fortification on any given site is also evidence that such a site originated with the fortification. In general this is most unlikely.

There is, however, another class of evidence which has been too little utilised, but which offers rich materials for the investigator, though it requires to be used with caution. This is the evidence of Scandinavian tradition itself, preserved in Scandinavian lands. This evidence makes it clear that the Scandinavian

[1] For a recent expression of the view of the paramount importance of Scandinavian influence in early Russia, see S. H. Cross, 'Mediaeval Russian Contacts with the West', in *Speculum*, Vol. x (1935), pp. 137f. The present writer cannot agree with Cross that 'The capacity of the outstanding princes of Kiev was...a product rather of Scandinavian energy than of Slavic inertia' (see 'Yaroslav the Wise', etc., *Speculum*, Vol. iv (1929), p. 197).   [2] *The Origin of the Ancient Rus* (London, 1877).

settlers went to Russian lands because these lands were known to be rich. The evidence of the Icelandic sagas points to organised centres of population in Russia already before the period of the great Viking settlements. It points to great wealth, especially in gold, and considerable military organisation before the arrival of the Norsemen. Such signs of a highly civilised life do not necessarily leave permanent material traces behind them, and unfortunately in Russia no written records of the pre-Scandinavian communities have come down to us. But the very presence of the Scandinavian kingdoms in Russia, and more especially the elaborate fortifications which they found it necessary to erect, imply the existence of such early wealthy pre-Norse communities, while an unbiased reading of even the *Povêst* itself indicates that traces of this early culture had by no means disappeared, even while Norse influence was at its height in Kiev. This will become clearer as we proceed.

Viewed in their true perspective the Scandinavians are merely an episode in Russian history, though admittedly a very important episode. It is not easy at the present time to gauge the exact proportion of the part which they played in northern Russia, owing to the absence of written records for the early period of Novgorod; but I have no doubt that when the importance of Norse literary records for Russian history comes to be more fully recognised, and when the results of Russian archaeological research are better known in the west, we shall be in a better position to fill in this blank sheet of a most interesting period. When this can be done it will probably be found that the influence of Sweden on northern Russia has been much stronger than that of the Scandinavian world in general on the south. For Sweden was at all times richer and more highly developed than Norway, and the trade route between Sweden and the Orient down the Volga was undoubtedly developed earlier than that of the Scandinavian world down the Dnêpr.[1] In all probability

---

[1] See F. Braun, 'Das historische Russland in Nordischen Schrifttum des x—xiv Jahrhunderts', in *Festschrift für Eugen Mogk* (Halle, 1924), pp. 150ff., and the references there cited. See especially T. J. Arne, *La Suède et l'Orient* (Uppsala, 1914).

the route up the Oka and down the Don and Donets was developed earlier than either, for we know that men calling themselves *Rus*, and claiming that their prince was known as *Chacanus* (*khagan*), were sent by the Greek Emperor Theophilos to the court of Louis le Débonnaire at Engelheim for repatriation to Sweden,[1] in 836, some ten or fifteen years before Ibn Khordadhbeh (†c. A.D. 912) describes the *Rus* merchants, whom he regards as 'some kind of Slavs', as journeying to the Black Sea, to the Khazar capital, to the Caspian, and even to Baghdad and eastern and southern Asia'. Ibn Rusta, writing in the beginning of the tenth century, but using, it is believed, a mid-ninth century source, tells us that 'the *Rus* have a ruler who is called *Khagan-Rus*'. But the term certainly points to those of the *Rus* who were in the proximity and under the influence of the Khazars, i.e. in all probability those on the lower Don.[2] It was probably the *Rus* of this region who supplied the Emperor Constantine V with ships to fight against the Bulgars in 773,[3] and it was probably the descendants of these same 'Rus' on the Sea of Azov who formed the nucleus later of Svyatoslav's principality with its capital at Tmutorakan on the Kuban River. In any case, there can be no doubt that the northern and eastern routes followed by the Norsemen certainly ran through a less fully developed region than that which passed through Kiev; and the number and wealth of the archaeological finds from northern and central Russia testify to the undoubted strength of Scandinavian cultural influence on this region.

But it cannot be too strongly emphasised that the history of Kiev is a palimpsest. It is an error to regard it as a Scandinavian development starting from zero. The traditions embodied in the *Povêst*, such as that of the early ferryman Kiy, and his importance for the early history of Kiev as a river port, reflect the period in which the Khazars must have been the paramount influence in

[1] *Annales Bertiniani, Mon. Germ.* I, 434.
[2] See further Vernadsky, *Ancient Russia* (Yale, 1943), pp. 280 f., 304 f.
[3] For references, see Vernadsky, *op. cit.* p. 279.

the neighbourhood. Ancient stone monuments in the environs of the city, but definitely outside the walls of Varangian Kiev, ancient sanctuary tradition associated with the hill overlooking the river—all these and many other hints in the pages of the *Povêst* recall an ancient civilised centre of the first importance, dating from Slav, or Khazar, or Gothic supremacy, or even from earlier times. How old civilisation may be at a place with the natural advantages of Kiev we cannot at present say.[1] We can, however, be sure that the Norse city already ruled by the Norsemen, Askold and Dir,[2] and conquered and refounded as a Norse colony by Oleg, is only a phase in the long history of an important emporium,[3] and that we are fortunate in our knowledge of this particular phase owing to the accident of a chronicler of the Slavonic revival having found it of interest for his purpose to demonstrate the foreign elements in the state of Kiev itself, above which his Slavonic heroes rose supreme, and led their people to a great national triumph against their foreign foes from without.

It is clear, therefore, that our quest of the beginnings of Russian history involves us in some very complex problems. Stated in their simplest terms these problems are, first, the nature of the history of Kiev prior to the composition of our earliest historical document, the chronicle composed in the reign of Monomakh; and secondly, the nature of the literary traditions which were still current in oral form at that time, and which purport to relate to the earlier period. What is the relationship of the second of these two problems to the first? Which of the two Vladimirs of whom

[1] Tripolye, about thirty miles south-east of Kiev, is believed to be one of the most ancient sites in Europe, being a Chalcolithic settlement.

[2] The Norse forms of these names would be Höskuldr and Dýri. The latter is very rare as a proper name in Scandinavian records. There was, however, a colonist in Iceland of this name. See *Landnámabók* (*Hauksbók* text), cap. III.

[3] On the continuity of the occupation and civilisation of the district of which Kiev forms the centre and focus, see M. Rostovtsev, *Iranians and Greeks in South Russia* (Oxford, 1922), pp. 210ff.; Vernadsky, *Ancient Russia*, p. 315; also *ib.* 'Lebedia', *Byzantion*, Vol. xiv (1939), p. 179.

traditions are recorded in the chronicle has been selected for oral transmission in the *byliny*? What is the basis of selection? What is the period which the oral traditions of the *byliny* have made their starting-point, and at what point do they imply that the age of the heroes is at an end?

I do not think that these problems can be solved without a careful study of the true historical position of the two Vladimirs, and of the conditions of their time. The facile assumption that Vladimir I was the last of the Norsemen, and the founder of the Russian state, and that this state was a Scandinavian colony, carries us nowhere. It fails to account for the original importance of either of the two Vladimirs, both in the true history of Russia, and also in the eyes of the earliest chronicler of this history; and it is contrary to the traditions contained in the *Povêst* itself, as we shall see. It is, moreover, contrary both to Scandinavian tradition, and to the well-authenticated history of the movements and motives of the Norsemen of the Viking Age in the west, and therefore in itself improbable as a theoretical reconstruction of their place in Russian history. On the other hand, the emphasis constantly laid in the annals of the *Povêst* on the importance of agriculture to the Slavs, especially in the neighbourhood of the large towns such as Kiev, forms the true background of the Norse invasions, and this must always have formed the warp and woof of the daily life of the people. The relics of Norse supremacy, best seen in legislation and technical matters relating to trade, are undoubtedly impressive and visible signs of the Viking Age in Russia. But the influence of the Norsemen must at all times have been virtually restricted to the towns, and the Norse rule in Russia, important though it is in regard to external relations, both peaceable and hostile, can never have had more than a secondary importance in the national life.

CHAPTER II

THE EARLY HISTORY OF KIEV

The account of early Russian history contained in the *Povêst* opens with antiquarian speculation based on the Biblical narrative of the division of the World among Shem, Ham and Japhet, and derives the Slavs from Japhet himself. The Slavs are described as dispersing from a single centre in their original home, which is here stated to have been on the Danube. This is followed by a passage —very interesting in its implications—which gives a brief account of the great river system of Russia, and its use as a network of what we might call trunk roads by which the Slavs obtained contact with the outside world. Next comes a very valuable account of the distribution and characteristics of the various Slavonic tribes, such as the Slavs on the middle Dnêpr, here described as Polians, 'the dwellers on the plains' (Russian *pole*, 'plain' or 'steppe'). Then come the Drevlians, 'the dwellers in the forest' (Russian *derevo*, 'tree'), immediately to the west, and the Dregovichi to the north-west, both of which tribes are described as being independent principalities. The Severians to the north are mentioned next, and many others follow. It is worth noting that the Slavs are described as already in existence as an independent principality at Novgorod at this early date. The Khazars are recognised as having dwelt to the east, while the Slavs were still on the Danube, and the successive sweeps over the plains of south Russia made by the Bulgars, the White Ugri [1] or Hungarians, the Avars, the Pechenegs, and the Black Ugri or Hungarians (i.e. Magyars), all from the eastern steppe, are briefly recorded.

The Polians are described as a number of small self-governing

---

[1] The chronicler identifies these with the Asiatic White Huns, saying that they attacked Khosroes; but the White Huns do not seem to have come into Russia. The Ugri are not Huns but Hungarians (Magyars).

units living peaceably together at this period. The chronicler then goes on to tell us that there were in early times three brothers known as Kiy, Shchek and Khoriv living on the middle Dnêpr, together with their sister Lybed.[1] The name of the latter is also that of a small tributary of the Dnêpr. Kiy and his brothers are said to have lived on three hills where Kiev now stands, and we are told that they built a town and named it Kiev after their eldest brother. The town is said to have been surrounded by pine forests inhabited by wild animals. The chronicler adds the interesting statement that people believed to be descended from these original Polians still lived in Kiev down to his own time. It is obvious that the names of the brothers and their sister are eponymous inventions, the result of antiquarian speculation; but the tradition that remnants of the earliest population still survived in Kiev in the writer's own day, despite the intermediate vicissitudes to which the place had been subjected, is interesting and probably true.

The chronicler tells us further that a tradition also existed in his day according to which Kiy was a ferryman, and that already in these far-off times a ferry had been in existence at the base of the hills on which stands the town of Kiev. The chronicler himself expresses scepticism in regard to the tradition on the ground that according to yet another tradition Kiy had made a journey to Tsargrad (Byzantium), and, as representative of his kindred, had been honourably received by the emperor—a statement incompatible with the simple status of a ferryman. Whatever these stories are worth, they at least indicate that Kiev was a very ancient place, far more ancient than is compatible with its origin as a Scandinavian settlement; that it owed its existence to the ferry, or to the easy crossing of the Dnêpr at this point, and therefore to trade; that it was of sufficient importance to have had relations, whether diplomatic or mercantile, with the Greek world; and that it formed a part of a local political organisation, developing peaceable relations with the neighbouring com-

[1] On Lybed or Lebed, see Vernadsky, *Byzantion*, Vol. XIV (1939), pp. 179ff.

munities as a part of a civilised unit. Whether this picture goes back to a Khazar or Gothic original, I am not competent to say, and it is to be doubted if we have at the present time sufficient data for determining the point. The name of one of the brothers, Shchek, is probably Turkish. But at least it can be definitely said that archaeological work in the neighbourhood of Kiev amply bears out the tradition of pre-Scandinavian settlement, and will doubtless in due course have much to tell us of the nature and period of the earlier occupants.

After the account of the founding of Kiev, the chronicler passes to an anthropological survey of the various peoples occupying the valley and head waters of the Dnêpr, including the Drevlians and the Polians themselves, after which he returns to the actual history of the Polians. These, we are told, were made tributary, after the deaths of the three brothers in Kiev, first to the Drevlians, and afterwards to the Khazars, and finally to the Varangians from beyond the sea. These Varangians are said to have first made the peoples of the north pay them tribute soon after the middle of the ninth century, but to have been ejected shortly afterwards. According to the testimony of the *Povêst*, however, anarchy followed their withdrawal, in consequence of which their former tributaries invited the Varangian 'Rus' to return and rule them. In answer to this request, three brothers bearing Norse names are said to have led migrations of the 'Rus' to northern Russia. The eldest, called Rurik (Old Norse Hraerekr), settled in Novgorod; the second, Sineus (O.N. Signjötr), in Bêlo-ozero; the third, Truvor (O.N. Thorvarthr),[1] in Izborsk; but the two latter are said to have died shortly afterwards, leaving Rurik as sole ruler of the north.[2] In this way, according to the testimony of the *Povêst*, begins the period of Scandinavian

[1] The word 'brothers' cannot be pressed. Thorvarthr, from his name, can hardly have been a *knyaz* or 'prince' but was almost certainly a *jarl*, Thor being the god to whom this class was devoted.

[2] For a recent discussion of his career, see Vernadsky, *Ancient Russia*, pp. 336 ff. Vernadsky accepts the view first put forward by Kruse in 1836, which identifies Rurik with Rurik of Jutland, born c. 800.

supremacy, the importance of which has been the subject of so much discussion and controversy.

When Rurik settled in the north, we are told that with him there were two men (*dva muzha*) who were not of his kin (*ne plemeniy ego*), but were *boyars*. The word *boyars* is doubtless used here to translate the Norse word *jarlar*, lit. 'earls', as distinct from the Norse *konungar*, 'kings', who in Scandinavia were numerous. The names of these two men were Askold (O.N. Höskuldr) and Dir (O.N. Dýri), and it is quite in accordance with early Teutonic tradition elsewhere that they act together as a pair of rulers, like Hengest and Horsa in our own country, like the early kings of Denmark in the traditions recorded by the Danish historian Saxo Grammaticus, and like the early Swedish princes in the traditions preserved by the Icelander, Snorri Sturluson, in the early traditional history of Sweden known as the *Ynglinga Saga*. Askold and Dir, we are told, obtained permission from Rurik to sail down the Dnêpr with the intention of visiting Tsargrad; but on arriving at Kiev, and learning that the city was tributary to the Khazars, they, together with their Varangian followers, took possession of it, and established themselves as supreme over the country of the Polians. We are told that they even attacked the Greeks, making a great massacre of the Christians and attacking Tsargrad with two hundred boats; but the flotilla, like so many other similar ventures, was scattered by a storm, and the survivors returned to their native land.

We need not regard the details of this story too seriously. Like other traditions of the Norsemen, it can neither be regarded as authentic history, nor dismissed as mere legend. Undoubtedly it reflects an early Scandinavian settlement in Kiev at an early date. The annal relating the attack on Byzantium is entered as between 863 and 866. The interest of the story lies in the tradition which it records that Kiev was settled by Scandinavians about the same time as Novgorod, and that its rulers were not of royal blood. This latter statement is worthy of careful consideration, for certain Norse sagas allow us to suspect that the later rulers of Kiev originated to the north of Trondhjem in Norway, a district which was not ruled by kings, like southern Norway and Sweden, but by hereditary landowners with wide territorial and political jurisdiction, some of whom were at least as powerful as the kings, like the *hersar* and *jarlar*, who scorned to assume the title of kings.[1] During and even after the Viking Age, this northern part of Norway was the home of many of the most intrepid and important families of adventurers and colonists. Here also, it will be remembered, was the home of the famous whaler Ohthere, whose visit to the court of Alfred the Great forms the most interesting entry in King Alfred's translation of Orosius' *History of the World*. It is by no means improbable, therefore, that Askold and Dir were of Hálogaland origin.

We are told that on the death of Rurik, some time between the years 870 and 879, Oleg succeeded him as ruler of Novgorod. Rurik, it is said, 'on his death-bed[2] bequeathed his realm to Oleg, who belonged to his kin (*ot roda êmu sushchu*), and he entrusted to his hands his son Igor (O.N. Yngvarr), for he was very young'. Later (903) it is said that as Igor grew up, he followed after Oleg, and 'obeyed his instruction'. A wife, Olga by name, was brought to him from Pskov. Who Olga was is not stated. According to a later source she is said to have been a Swedish princess. Her name and her connection with Oleg, however, suggest that she was his own daughter. The name Oleg corresponds to Norse Helgi, while Olga, which appears in the Norse sagas of the period as Allogia, represents the earlier form Helga,[3] the feminine of Helgi. Oleg is described as Igor's 'fosterer' or guardian, and Oleg's responsibility in regard to the upbringing

[1] An example is the famous Jarl Guthbrandr of the Dales, whose territories lay in the mountain district to the south-east of the Trondhjem Fjord. He and his family were great upholders of the cult of the god Thor, the god chiefly worshipped by the class of *bændr* or small landowners, as distinct from the cult of Óthinn, which was chiefly patronised by the court of King Harold the Fair-haired in the south.

[2] The translation is doubtful, as the construction of the Russian sentence is curious. The form used is *umershyu*, a past participle.

[3] Her name appears in the contemporary notice by Constantine Porphyrogenitos as Ἔλγα (cf. p. 31 below).

of Igor suggests that the young prince was handed over to him
by his father for fosterage in accordance with an ancient and
widespread Scandinavian institution.[1] It would be fully in accordance with what the Norse sagas have to tell us as to this
institution that Oleg should hand over the young prince to his
own daughter to be brought up, and that some preliminary form
of marriage should take place between them, even in Igor's
extreme youth.[2]

Shortly after the death of Rurik, Oleg won Kiev on behalf
of Igor by the following stratagem. Coming to the hills of Kiev,
and finding Askold and Dir ruling there, he hid his warriors in
boats, left some others behind, and went forward himself, bearing
the child Igor. He thus came to the foot of the ' Magyars' Hill'
(*Ugorskoe*),[3] and after concealing his troops, he sent messengers
to Askold and Dir, representing himself as a stranger on his way
to Greece, and bidding them come forward to meet their fellow-
countrymen. When Askold and Dir came out, the men jumped
out of the boats and killed them, and buried them on the same
hill, 'and churches were built on the spot', whatever that may
signify. Oleg, it is added, ruled in Kiev, and the princes of
Novgorod, Chernigov, Pereyaslavl, Polotsk, Rostov and Lyu-
bech were subject to him. He established his authority over
the Polians and the Drevlians on the middle Dnêpr, and over
the Severians and the Radimichi farther north, forbidding the
two latter to continue their tribute to the Khazars. He is said,
moreover, to have been at war with the Uluchi and the
Tivertsy.

The most important feat attributed to him is a successful raid
against Byzantium between the years 904 and 907, as a result of

---

[1] The usual word in Norse for an older man who fulfils the function of
guardian or foster-parent for the son of an equal is *fóstri*, and the same
function seems to belong to the Russian *kormilets*, a word which is frequently used in the *Povêst*.

[2] I have dealt with this subject of fosterage more fully elsewhere in a
forthcoming book on early Norse religious tradition.

[3] The hill so-called later from the passage of the Magyars.

which he is said to have forced the Greek emperor to form a treaty with him in 907. In this expedition he is said to have been accompanied by a large number of the tribes of northern and western Russia, including his old enemies the Tivertsy. With these he made his way southwards with horses and ships, and ravaged and burnt the suburbs of Byzantium. He is said to have been known as Oleg *Vêshchi*, 'Oleg the Wise', but 'wise' in the sense denoting supernatural or uncanny wisdom.[1]

The circumstances under which Oleg's treaty with the Greeks was implemented are worthy of note. We are told that he sent envoys to Byzantium to the Emperor Leo VI, who honoured them with rich gifts, and who 'placed his retainers at their disposal to show them the beauties of the churches, the golden palace, and the riches contained therein'—a delightful picture of a courteous host showing the sights of a great city to strangers. It is also stated that they 'instructed the Russes in their faith, and expounded to them the true belief', after which they returned to Kiev with great honour. We shall have occasion to return again later to this early intimation of knowledge of the Christian faith in Kiev.

The death of Oleg is one of the most picturesque incidents in the *Povêst*, and it is also important for the close similarity which it bears to another incident in ancient Norse saga to which I shall have occasion to refer later. I will therefore quote the story of the death of Oleg in full in the words of the *Povêst* itself.

'Now Autumn came on, and Oleg bethought him of his horse which he had ordered to be fed, yet not mounted. For he had made enquiry of the wonder-working magicians: "From what shall death come to me?" One magician replied: "O, Prince, the steed which you love and on which you ride, from him you shall meet your death." Oleg then took this to heart and said: "Never shall I mount him or look upon him again." So he gave command that the horse should be properly fed, but never led into his presence. He thus let several years pass not seeing him

[1] The word is to be distinguished from *mudry*, 'wise', in the sense of wisdom as we understand the term.

until he attacked the Greeks. And having returned to Kiev, and having passed four years, on the fifth he thought of the horse through whom the magicians had foretold that he should meet his death. He thus summoned his head groom, and enquired as to the whereabouts of the horse which he had ordered to be fed and well cared for. The groom answered that he was dead. Oleg laughed and mocked the magicians, exclaiming: "Sooth-sayers tell untruths, and their words are naught but falsehood. The horse is dead, but I am still alive."

'Then he commanded that a horse should be saddled. "Let me see his bones", said he. He rode to the place where the bare bones and the skull lay. Dismounting from his horse, he laughed and remarked: "Am I to receive my death from this skull?" and he stamped upon the skull with his foot. But a serpent crawled forth from it and bit him in the foot, so that in consequence he sickened and died. All the people mourned for him in great grief. They bore him away and buried him on the hill which is called Shchekovitsa. His tomb is there to this day. It is called the Tomb of Oleg.'[1]

Such, stated in the briefest terms, is what the Russian records have to tell us of the earliest history of Kiev, and of the dawn of the history of Russia as a state. It is clear that this history is already ancient before the arrival of the Scandinavians, and that both in the valley of the Dnêpr, and in the north and east, civilised and highly developed communities were living in more or less close touch with the Greek world at an early date. The record of the *Povêst*, interpreted in the light of what the Scandinavian sagas have to tell us of conditions in Scandinavia itself, suggests that while Novgorod was included in Swedish territory by a gradual process of diplomatic and mercantile arrangement, and ruled over by a royal line, Kiev was brought under Norse rule directly from Hálogaland,[2] possibly as the result of a gradual growth as a trading outpost, but ruled, not by kings, but by hereditary land-

[1] *Povêst*, transl. Cross, p. 158.
[2] The route from Hálogaland may have led through Sweden, but this is not necessarily the case.

owners like parts of Hálogaland itself, and other parts of central and northern Norway. The fact that two rulers are named at the earliest period of Kiev under Scandinavian rule, and that these are represented as ruling simultaneously at the outset, stamps the tradition at once as Teutonic, and not the result of Slavonic antiquarian speculation. It is to be suspected that Sineus and Truvor, who are represented as both dying two years after their arrival, are of similar origin, and perhaps unconnected with Rurik, whose 'pair' (cf. p. 20 above) would seem to have been Oleg himself.

It would, I think, be a mistake to dismiss the reign of Oleg as mythical on the ground that it has not hitherto been possible to identify him with any of the more prominent men known to us from the Scandinavian sagas. Even the story of his raid on Byzantium can hardly be dismissed as 'apocryphal' on the ground that no reference is made to it in Greek sources. On the other hand there can be no doubt that this part of the *Povêst* is derived wholly or almost wholly from oral tradition, and as such cannot be treated as if it were history. The two types of record—oral tradition and historical documents—are quite different, and require to be handled in very different ways; but both are deserving of a respectful regard, and oral tradition only comes to be despised as a source of history when this distinction is not fully recognised. It would be as grave an error to treat these early annals of the *Povêst* as historical in the strict sense of the word as it would be to dismiss them as devoid of historical value. It seems to me extremely probable that the story of Oleg's attack on Byzantium, and of his treaty with the Greeks, reflects certain historical facts, though these facts have become distorted by the oral medium through which they have passed. I shall return to this subject later.

In discussing the milieu of Oleg here, however, I should like to call attention once more—many have done it before me—to the close similarity of the story of his death to that of the Norse (Hálogaland) hero Örvar-Oddr. According to the Norse saga, which occurs in the collection known as the *Fornaldar Sögur*

Northrlanda,[1] Oddr had scorned the prophecies of a *völva*, or 'prophetess', and the *völva* had retaliated by prophesying that Oddr should be slain by his horse Faxi. In order to avert the curse, Faxi was killed, and a barrow was raised over him; but towards the end of his life, Oddr decided to return from his travels and to visit his home in Norway. On his return journey, he went to look at Faxi's grave mound, and while he was there an adder sprang out from his horse's skull and bit him so that he died, thus fulfilling the *völva*'s prophecy. It has been shown[2] that neither the story of Oleg nor that of Örvar-Oddr belonged originally to either hero, but that they represent a current story which may have had its origin in Turkish sources. It may, however, be taken as probable that the motif has been introduced into the stories of the Russian and the Norse heroes owing to some resemblance which it bears to traditions originally associated with these heroes.

It may be added that the career of the early Russian ruler Oleg, as we find it in the pages of the *Povêst*, has much in common with that of the Norse hero Örvar-Oddr, in addition to the virtually identical accounts of their deaths. It would be tedious to enter into details here as to the similarities of the two accounts. It may however be mentioned that Oddr, like Oleg, made a journey to Russia at an early date, which made him famous all his life, and earned him the nickname Oddr Víthförli, 'Oddr the Far-travelling'. Like Oleg he first went to northern Russia, and later to the south, and like Oleg's his longest and greatest journey was to the east. He seems to have been the most renowned man of his time, and his saga tells us more of the historical geography of Russia in his day than any other saga. The ruler of *Holmgarthr* (Novgorod) is represented in this saga as jealous of the Russian depredations of Oddr in early life, and of his prestige later, and

[1] Ed. Rafn, Copenhagen, 3 vols., 1829–1830; also V. Ásmundarson, Reykjavík, 1886–1891; also a critical annotated edition by R. C. Boer, *Örvar-Odds Saga* (Halle a.S., 1892).

[2] A. Stender-Petersen, *Die Varägersage als Quelle der Altrussischen Chronik* (Leipzig, 1934), pp. 176 ff.

a lifelong rivalry and feud existed between the two men, which was, however, patched up towards the end of their lives.

Before leaving the subject of Oleg it may be pointed out that a large proportion of the proper names which occur as the signatories of his so-called treaty with the Greeks are not those commonly current in the Viking Age, but are found in the oral records of previous times. In particular it may be mentioned that some of the names which we associate with the earlier period are found in the saga of Örvar-Oddr. Thus the name Ingjaldr is the name of Oddr's 'fosterer'; Vermundr is the name of his nephew; Hróarr and Gunnarr appear on a collateral line of his family tree. In addition to these names which occur in the treaty, it may be mentioned that Ásmundr, the name of Svyatoslav's *kormilets*, or 'fosterer', is also the name of the son of Ingjaldr, Oddr's foster-father. I should not like to lay much weight on these coincidences in view of the fact that all the names mentioned are known elsewhere from heroic poetry; but the coincidences are worth mentioning in view of the fact that the range of these names is completely different from that of the names in the later treaties, and suggests that they are of a different origin. I shall return to this subject later.

The beginning of Igor's reign is placed in annal 913, and his death in annal 945.[1] The chief events are his war against the Drevlians, which began at the outset of his reign, and which seems to have turned on the matter of tribute; and his attack on Byzantium. With the new scourge which appeared on the Russian plains in 915 in the form of the Pechenegs, Igor also appears to have found himself in difficulties. For though he is said to have made peace with them so that they turned southwards towards the Danube, we read in one text (the Hypatian) of the *Povêst* that he was at war with them at some period between 916 and 920.

Igor's first attack on the Greeks is related in the entry 935–941. This seems to have been in the nature of a raid on the grand scale against the Greek villages on the shores of the Black Sea.

[1] The chronology of Igor's reign is difficult to accept as it stands. See Laehr, *Die Anfänge des russischen Reiches* (Berlin, 1930), p. 129.

The Greek emperor dispersed it with 'Greek fire', and the remnants of Igor's forces returned home; but in 944 Igor had collected a much more formidable expedition, including many of the northern tribes, and even the Pechenegs themselves, with whom he seems at this point to have made an alliance. He is said to have advanced with both ships and horses, denoting no doubt his Varangian and his Pecheneg forces respectively. This time the Greek emperor bought off both Igor and his Pecheneg allies with gold, ratifying the peace with an elaborate treaty which we shall discuss more fully later.

The Pechenegs had doubtless been induced to take part in the expedition with confident hope of the gold which, in fact, they actually acquired as a result of it. We need not doubt that the Pecheneg alliance would be a costly one for Igor, and it may well have been the cause of his attack against the Drevlians in 945, the avowed object of which was to increase the tribute already paid to the Russes under Oleg. Igor's followers are represented as having encouraged him to make the attack, pointing out to him, according to the picturesque narrative with which the *Povêst* abounds at this early period, that the servants of his *voevoda* Sveinald were better clad than themselves; but the Drevlians likened him to a ravening wolf, and slew him near the city Izkorosten.

After the death of Igor, his wife Olga, we are told (s.a. 945), was in Kiev with her son Svyatoslav, whose tutor, or, as we should say in Norse terminology, whose *fóstri*, was one Asmund (O.N. Ásmundr).[1] The Drevlians are said to have sent a deputation of twenty of their picked men in a boat to sue for the hand of Olga for their prince. The description given by the chronicle of this event is of exceptional interest, in regard both to the event itself, and also to the site. The prince's *dvor* ('court'),[2] we are told,

---

[1] *Ás-* is O.N. for 'a god', and *mundr* is O.N .for 'a pledge'. The name itself is very much like the O.N. name *Guthmundr*, which has the same root meaning. *Ásmundr* is also the name of the foster-brother of Örvar-Oddr, the son of his *fóstri*, Ingjaldr.

[2] The word in the text is *dvor*, of which the closest equivalent would be the German word *hof*, i.e. a spacious house with its courtyard.

was inside the city of Kiev, which was on high ground above the river, and it is added that the inhabitants of Kiev did not live in the valley, but in the city above. Nevertheless it is expressly stated that outside the city of Kiev there was another *dvor*. This was a *dvor* ('inhabited building') with a *terem* ('high chamber'), and this *terem* was of stone. These details, which are so curiously insisted on by the chronicler, appear pointless in the story as it stands; but the site near the bank of the river (still known as *podol*), outside the city, not in the actual occupied area of Kiev itself, yet obviously occupied by an important stone building, recalls the stone barrows of the Norse sagas, erected not far from the royal dwellings, both in Sweden and Norway, which seem to have combined the functions of sanctuary and tomb, and to have been frequently placed near the seashore.

The story goes on to relate that Olga feigned acceptance of the suit of the Drevlians, bidding them come again on the following day, not on horseback, nor on foot, but in their boat. She then gave command that a large deep trench (*yama*) should be dug in the *dvor* with the *terem* outside the city. Then she seated herself in the *terem* to await the arrival of the Drevlians, much as we shall see Vladimir I awaiting the arrival of Yaropolk at a later date. The Drevlians were carried into the *dvor* in their boat, 'seated on the cross benches (?)[1] in flowing robes, puffed up with pride', and then dropped into the deep trench. Olga then had them buried alive.

Here indeed are a 'ship burial' and a human sacrifice on the grand scale, performed by a wife for the death of her husband. The scene is strikingly reminiscent of many ship burials in stone barrows on the edge of the sea described in the Norse sagas. In such stories it is sometimes said that a man builds for himself a barrow during his lifetime, and that he enters it while he is still alive with all his ship's crew. Frequently in these sagas we read of the Norse heroes breaking into such barrows, and finding a ship fully manned with a crew richly dressed and laden with treasure, seated, like the Drevlians, on the cross benches. It is possible that Igor had built the barrow for himself during his

[1] The meaning appears to be doubtful.

own lifetime, like other Swedish princes; and that Olga, seated there in state awaiting the Drevlians, is performing some form of ritual substitute for suttee, like other Swedish princesses of the period.

Other stories are told in the *Povêst* of Olga's vengeance against the Drevlians. According to one of these a second embassy of picked men whom the Drevlians sent to Kiev was enticed on its arrival into a heated bath house and thus burnt to death. The story has the appearance of being a variant of the ship burial. It is, indeed, not impossible that both stories embody a partial version of the original tradition, which may possibly have approximated to another story related by the Arabic traveller and geographer, Ibn Faḍlān, of the burning of another 'Rus' funeral ship on the Volga about the year 921. Be that as it may, it is possible that Olga, as a true Scandinavian, owed some form of suttee, whether actual or ritual, to her husband. And in this connection we may note both the exacting nature of the vengeance which she took on the Drevlians in burning the town of Izkorosten where Igor lay buried, and also the heavy tribute which she laid upon them. We hear nothing in her day of the Pechenegs; but it is probable that the heavy tribute which both Olga and Igor insisted on exacting from the Drevlians was sorely needed by them to purchase immunity from the nomads, especially in view of Olga's projected journey to Tsargrad.

The entire story of Olga's relations with the Drevlians reads exactly like a Norse saga. In view of this it is tempting to see in her journey to Tsargrad a device for evading suttee in some form or other. The journey as it stands in the *Povêst* follows hard upon her vengeance for her husband, but is wholly unmotivated in the *Povêst*. It is strongly to be suspected that the true object of the journey and of her zeal for baptism was to escape the old heathen observance of burial alive, if only temporarily, in the husband's barrow. An additional incentive, if any were needed, to evade suttee might lie in the extreme youth of her son Svyatoslav at this time.

This is, of course, merely a suggested possibility. It is indeed not generally recognised that suttee was ever at all common in Scandinavia, though I think that there can be no doubt that, in Sweden at least, and probably in Norway also, it formed an important part of early ritual, and I have examined this subject more fully elsewhere.[1] Even if it is admitted that suttee was a recognised duty of a wife, it cannot be said to be at all certain that Olga concerned herself in any way with the matter. Yet on the whole I think that the evidence seems to suggest that this was so. It is significant that her son Svyatoslav refused to follow her example in becoming a Christian, and that she never forced him in any way to do so. It is indeed possible that if Olga's conversion was in any degree inspired by such a motif as I have suggested, it may have been connected with a reaction against the practice in the latter half of the tenth century; for some thirty years after Olga's day we find Sigríthr the Proud insisting on divorce from her husband King Eiríkr of Sweden, because it was, we are told, a law of the Swedish kings that their wives should be placed beside them in the barrow, and she did not wish to be condemned to such a fate.[2]

The rest of the reign of Olga is occupied in the annals of the *Povêst* with an account of her journey to Tsargrad, and forms a sober and dignified narrative,[3] such as we should expect to find in relation to an early convert to the Greek Church, and a queen. We have, in fact, two totally different types of evidence relating to Olga. The first, which is clearly based on Scandinavian saga, represents her as a zealous heathen, and a passionate and vigorous woman such as we find frequently in the sagas of Iceland. The second, which is doubtless directly derived from some written Life, probably of Greek provenance, is a piece of hagiology which describes her as an Orthodox Christian, and a highly intellectual

[1] In the forthcoming book referred to on p. 22 above.
[2] *Flâteyjarbók*, Vol. I, 'Saga of Olaf Tryggvason', ch. 63.
[3] We have the Greek official contemporary record of her visit to Tsargrad, or Byzantium, in the work of Constantine Porphyrogenitos, *De Ceremoniis Aulae Byzantinae* (Bonn, 1829), II. 15 (pp. 594 ff.), where her name is given as Ἔλγα.

woman with a sense of the importance of statecraft and the value of political institutions.

Svyatoslav, the son of Igor and Olga, is the most heroic figure of what is generally known as the Norse period of early Russian history; and the entries in the *Povêst* relating to his early warfare and conquests are of a totally different nature from those which we have been discussing. They suggest that they are derived, at least in part, from early panegyric poetry rather than from saga. They abound in brilliant similes, short and summary statements of startling achievements, and brief and pointed speeches. The opening annal (956–967) reads like an echo of the Norse *Hrafns-mál*, a brief panegyric poem by a Norse *skald*, or court poet, composed on King Harold the Fair-haired: 'Stepping light as a leopard, he [i.e. Svyatoslav] undertook many campaigns. Upon his expeditions he carried with him neither wagons nor kettles, and boiled no meat, but cut off small strips of horse-flesh, game or beef, and ate it after roasting it on the coals. Nor did he have a tent, but spread out a garment under him, and set his saddle under his head, and all his retinue did likewise.'

This and the following entries, enumerating briefly his campaigns and victories over the surrounding peoples, recall the Norse poem *Glymdrápa*, composed by the *skald* Thorbjörn Hornklofi, which enumerates King Harold's campaigns and victories.

To judge from the records, Svyatoslav would be just the kind of prince to attract a devoted *druzhina*, and to inspire the encomia of a school of skaldic poetry. His conquests are on the grand scale; not the small tribes in the valley of the Dnêpr, but the Vyatichians to the north-east, the Khazars with their stone Byzantine built fortress at Sarkel on the Don, and also the Kasogs[1] to the east and south, the Bulgarians on the Danube. Leaving Olga in charge of Kiev, he is said to have established his headquarters at Pereyaslavets on the Danube, from where he was able to treat with the Greek emperor. In his absence the

[1] I.e. the present Circassians; see V. Minorsky, *Hudud al-ʻAlam* (London, 1937), p. 446; cf. *Encyclopaedia of Islam*, s.v. *Kuban*.

Pechenegs laid siege to Kiev, and succeeded in cutting off the people of the city from the 'Rus' army on the other side of the Dnêpr. The siege was eventually raised by Svyatoslav's *voevoda* Prêtich, who induced the Pechenegs to withdraw, and eventually Svyatoslav, who marched to the scene from the Danube, forced the Pechenegs to keep their distance in the southern steppes, and to leave the neighbourhood of Kiev.

In this part of the life of Svyatoslav we have passed from the panegyric to the narrative style. In the account of the siege and relief of Kiev, and the escape of Olga and her two sons across the river, the negotiations between Prêtich and the Pecheneg prince, and the final return of Svyatoslav, who, it is said, 'bestrode his charger and returned to Kiev with his *druzhina*', is a perfect short story in the form of a *slovo* or short saga, and it may well be based on this form of literary historical record current in the time of the chronicler.

After the departure of the Pechenegs from the neighbourhood of Kiev, and the death of Olga immediately afterwards, Svyatoslav marched south and recaptured Pereyaslavets on the Danube from the Bulgars, using it as a base from which to menace the Greek cities and march against the capital. At first he appears to have been victorious, and the emperor made offers of tribute which Svyatoslav accepted, withdrawing his troops, which are said to have been close to Tsargrad, and returning with much glory to Pereyaslavets. A formal treaty followed between the Greeks and the 'Rus', of which the text is included in the *Povêst*, s.a. 971, and to which we shall return later. The following year Svyatoslav was killed by the Pechenegs as he was navigating the cataracts of the Dnêpr on his return to Kiev. It is noteworthy that his *voevoda* Sveinald had advised him to make a détour on horseback, in order to avoid the Pecheneg menace, and that it was by refusing to follow this advice that the prince met his death. Sveinald himself returned to Kiev.

The story of Svyatoslav's relations with the Greeks, like that of the siege of Kiev by the Pechenegs, forms a well-knit unit, a complete short story in itself, with fully related speeches, and vivid and picturesque details. It is saga, but sober and dignified saga such as we find in the medieval *slovesa* like the *Zadonshchina*, and quite unlike the bizarre and fantastic stories of Olga's early relations with the Drevlians, which resemble closely the Norse sagas of an apparently unhistorical character known as *Fornaldar Sögur*. These two *slovesa* of Svyatoslav may well be derived ultimately from contemporary panegyrics on the prince, composed by minstrels of his *druzhina*; but it seems to me on the whole more probable, comparing them with other examples of early *slovesa* which have survived,[1] that they represent an independent form of oral literature, a stage intermediate between the panegyric and the extended saga, constituting a brief narrative in highly coloured artificial prose, capable of easy and ready memorisation and transmission in a somewhat fluid state, but within limits closely fixed by the extent and scope of the subject.

Little is told us of Svyatoslav's son and successor, Yaropolk, save his feud with his brothers, Oleg and Vladimir; but the story, brief though it is, is full of interest and significance for the light which it throws on the influence of the *voevodas*, and the important though somewhat elusive role played by the Drevlians in the early history of Kiev. Yaropolk's reign begins in the year 973 ; and in the following year we are told that his brother Oleg, while hunting wild beasts in the forests west of Kiev, came accidentally on one Lyut, the son of the *voevoda* Sveinald, who was also hunting there. Oleg rode up to him, and enquired who he was, and on learning that he was a son of Sveinald, he rode up to him and killed him, 'for', adds the chronicler, 'Oleg was hunting too'. It will be noticed that Oleg's act is a deliberate piece of hostility directed against Sveinald, his father's *voevoda*; but whether because Sveinald had given his support to Yaropolk rather than to Oleg himself, or whether because Oleg naturally challenged Sveinald's rights in Drevlian territory,[2] is not clear.

[1] A fuller discussion of early Russian *slovesa* will be found in my chapter on Russian oral saga in *The Growth of Literature*, Vol. II (Cambridge, 1936), pp. 164 ff.

[2] In annal 6478 (A.D. 970) we are told that Svyatoslav had assigned the Drevlian territory to Oleg.

It is, however, clear that some previous feud evidently existed between Svyatoslav's *voevoda* and Oleg. When therefore we are told that a feud sprang up between Yaropolk and Oleg, and that 'Sveinald was continually egging Yaropolk on to attack his brother and seize his property because he wished to avenge his son', we may suspect that some motive even deeper and older than desire for vengeance underlay Sveinald's policy.

What follows makes it clear that Oleg had some reason to regard Dereva as his own preserve. The city of Vruchi near Izkorosten is referred to as his own possession, and there can be little doubt that this district had been assigned to him, either by Svyatoslav or by Yaropolk on his accession. In the following year (s.a. 976–977) Yaropolk marched into Dereva against Oleg, who was defeated and killed as he was seeking refuge in Vruchi, where his grandfather Igor lay buried. The story of the battle and of the death of Oleg is vividly described in words which are curiously reminiscent of Lithuanian oral epic poetry,[1] and which may even have left echoes in the Russian *bylina* of Sukhan Domantevich. The result of the battle was to leave Yaropolk supreme ruler for the moment, for his half-brother Vladimir, on hearing of the death of Oleg, 'fled abroad', and Yaropolk appointed his own *posadniki* ('governors', or 'mayors') in Novgorod.

Who these *posadniki* are we are not told, but it is strongly to be suspected from what follows that they are Dobrynya and Sveinald, and that the two latter are Drevlians. Whether Vladimir had been sojourning during his absence in Dereva or in Scandinavia is not clear; but while the former was his mother's native country, we know that he returned to Novgorod shortly after the events just recorded with Varangian allies. From what follows, however, it is clear that he owed his rise to power to both Drevlian and Norse supporters, and his first act of policy was the marriage which he succeeded in effecting with Rogned (O.N. Ragnheithr), the daughter of Rogvolod, prince of Polotsk,

---

[1] See, e.g., the poems published by M. Biržiška, *Dainu Atsiminimai iš Lietuvos Istorijos* (Vilna, 1920).

who had been about to marry his brother Yaropolk—himself already married to a Greek nun who had been brought home by his father Svyatoslav. This early Norse alliance was an act of statesmanship on the part of a son of a Russian father and a Drevlian mother, who was nevertheless depending for the moment on the support of a Varangian army.

The reign of Yaropolk, which began in 973, was short, and no stories are preserved save that of his death at the hands of his brother Vladimir. This is related from the point of view, not of Yaropolk, but of Vladimir himself, who, as the reputed founder of the Russian Church, claims the sympathy of the chronicler. The murder of Yaropolk is accordingly represented as a piece of treachery on the part of Blud, Yaropolk's *voevoda* in Kiev, who is possibly the 'governor', whom, we are told, he had left previously in Novgorod, and who had subsequently been dispatched to him by Vladimir with a challenge to battle. The part played by Blud is represented by the chronicler as a response to overtures and promises made to him by Vladimir; but it is probable that his motives lay deeper, and that his policy was dictated by a desire to overthrow Yaropolk as being a direct representative of the Norse dynasty, and to instate Vladimir in his place. Vladimir's sympathies were, as we shall see, wholly Slavonic, and more especially Drevlian. Always behind the early annals of the *Povêst* we are aware of the shadowy power of the Drevlian principality moving the pawns on the Dnêpr as pieces in the game of politics.

The story of the actual murder of Yaropolk is a curious one. On the advice of Blud he had fled from Kiev, and Vladimir had occupied the city, whereupon Blud undertook to bring Yaropolk into his presence. Vladimir, we are told, on hearing this, 'went to his father's *dvor* with the *terem*, of which we have previously made mention, and settled there with his retinue'. Yaropolk arrived in Vladimir's presence, though warned of Vladimir's treachery by a certain Varyazhko, whose name[1] suggests that he was probably the leader of Yaropolk's Varangian guard in Kiev,

[1] The name is a diminutive of *Varyag-*, 'the Varangian'.

and who urged him to flee to the Pechenegs. As Yaropolk
entered his brother's presence two Varangians stabbed him under
the arms with their swords, while Blud shut the doors to prevent
his men from following him in. The Varangians seem to have
acted from mercenary motives, for we are told that they subsequently made representations to Vladimir that they had won
the city themselves, and were therefore entitled to the taxes; and
it is probable that Yaropolk, like his predecessors and successors,
had found himself short of funds wherewith to pay his Varangian
army in Kiev, or to buy off the Pechenegs, as soon as he had
alienated the Drevlians. Varyazhko himself fled to the Pechenegs,
with whom Yaropolk was doubtless in some form of alliance.

In this tangle of politics and intrigue, the part played by Blud
stands out clearly. Yaropolk's *voevoda* had become alienated, and
consequently gave his loyalty to Vladimir. No motive is stated;
but Blud's non-Norse name, and the hints which are not lacking
of Yaropolk's connection with the Pechenegs, suggest that Blud
himself was actuated by patriotic motives, that his policy was
pro-Slavonic and anti-Pecheneg. It would be natural to suppose
that Blud saw in Vladimir, with his Drevlian background, and
his strongly Slavonic sympathies and Norse military support and
marriage alliance, the best hope for the future of Kiev against the
ever-present Pecheneg menace. In this he proved himself to be
a wise and far-seeing politician.

The actual nature of Yaropolk's death is extremely puzzling.
It is related with an amount of circumstantial detail which
suggests that it had been celebrated in oral literary form. The
actual murder is said to have been performed by Scandinavians.
It took place in the same building in which, according to tradition,
Olga had made the living sacrifice of the Drevlians in their ship,
burying them alive. The murder of Yaropolk was effected by a
double stabbing within the building, and the door was immediately shut on the heels of the king. He had been warned previously by a Norseman that his death was intended if he entered
the building. His death, therefore, has all the appearance of a
ritual sacrifice, possibly even of some form of giving of himself

to Othinn by entering alive into the tomb, the door of which immediately shut on his heels, just as we find in certain Norse sagas in which there are many examples of this form of euthanasia.

It would, of course, be a mistake to press too closely such an interpretation of the scene just enacted; but there can be no doubt that the chronicler has not always succeeded in interpreting correctly the actions and motives, and especially anything in the nature of the ritual or institutions which he is recording. This is especially evident when he is describing customs of the Drevlians or Scandinavians. It is just possible that the inability of the monastic chronicler to understand the customs of non-Slavonic populations which may come under his consideration may help to account for the fantastic picture which he draws of Vladimir's relations with women. This is no doubt partly accounted for by his desire to throw into high light the contrast of Vladimir's behaviour after his conversion, and it is also, of course, coloured by the example of the Biblical Solomon, which the chronicler evidently regards as relevant.

But there must have been some nucleus of fact to account for his evident anxiety to set the matter forth in the right light. The explanation doubtless lies in Vladimir's diplomatic marriages. The chronicler may well have been shocked by a king who counted among his wives women of Greek, Norse, Czech, and other nationalities, perhaps living also in a number of different places. Doubtless Vladimir, with his series of wives, appeared to him as a monster of vice. Yet if the picture is to be trusted at all, if indeed Vladimir did possess a number of wives at once, as is not at all improbable, such a state of things would not be in any way a violation of accepted custom and good behaviour in certain areas and among certain peoples. Thus we find in the stories contained in the early Norse *Flateyjarbók* that, according to Norse saga tradition, Jarl Hákon of Hlathir in Norway, who was a contemporary of Vladimir shortly before 1000, was inordinately fond of women and visited them in their paternal homes. Yet a careful reading of the saga leaves little room to doubt that Jarl Hákon in this matter was correctly following established custom in early Scandinavia, and that it was in the best interests of the women that after marriage they and their children should continue to live on in the woman's paternal home, visited by their husbands from time to time. It is probably in the light of what the chronicler has previously described as Drevlian promiscuity, and of such Norse usage as that referred to above, that we ought to interpret the stories of the marriage alliances of Vladimir, and his behaviour in regard to women.

CHAPTER III

GREEK AND ORIENTAL EVIDENCE

We must now turn to outside records to see how far it is possible to obtain further light on the events recorded in the Russian chronicle. Apart from the Norse sagas, the chief sources of information are the records of the contemporary Greek writers living in Byzantium. These Greek records are very valuable, being often full and detailed, and at times drawn from people who were the eyewitnesses of the events which they describe. Arabic accounts are almost equally valuable, being also derived in part from eyewitnesses, and being at times even fuller than the Greek. Some of these were also written in Byzantium itself. These Arabic accounts have a special importance, partly as being first-hand accounts of the Norsemen at their most easterly limit, and partly because, unlike the accounts of the western Vikings, which are derived mainly from the Icelandic sagas, and as such have passed through a literary medium intended·for purposes of entertainment, these eastern accounts are much closer to our modern ideas of historical writing. They have, in addition, the advantage over the western records of having been committed to writing either absolutely contemporaneously with the events recorded, or comparatively shortly afterwards.

Finally, we have a small but extremely interesting document relating to the Khazars which is also relevant to our study. This document is one of a small group of documents composed in the Hebrew language, and purporting to relate to the Khazars of the tenth century. They have been recently re-edited and published with photographic facsimile and exhaustive notes by the Russian scholar Kokovtsov,[1] and consist of a letter purporting to be by

[1] P. K. Kokovtsov, *Evreisko-Khazarskaia Perepiska v. X Veke* (*A Hebrew-Khazar Correspondence of the Tenth Century*; in Russian, Leningrad, 1932). The value of Kokovtsov's work for a thorough study and investigation of the documents in question is admitted by all scholars, even those who, like Grégoire, are not in agreement with his conclusions.

a Spanish Jew named Hasdai Ibn Shafrut or Shapperut to the Khazar king Joseph, and relating to a period some time before 960; King Joseph's answer, of which two versions are extant; and the document in which we are especially interested, and which appears to be a fragment of a letter or narrative from an unknown Khazar Jew. This fragment, which was discovered by Schechter, and first published by him in 1912,[1] is at present in the Cambridge University Library (T. S. Loan, 38), and is commonly referred to in discussions relating to these Khazar documents as the 'Cambridge Document'.

The authenticity of these documents, and more especially of the Cambridge fragment, which is the one which concerns us more directly, and the correct reading of the proper names which it contains, have given rise to much controversy, and the last word on the matter has not yet been spoken. The chief sceptic was the late J. Marquart; but a recrudescence of scepticism in an extreme form is represented by an article by H. Grégoire in *Byzantion*, Vol. XII (1937), pp. 225 ff. Still more recently M. Landau, after a detailed examination of the text, is said to have come to the conclusion that the Cambridge fragment, as well as the letter to Joseph, are both authentic.[2] Kokovtsov's treatment is the fullest and most scholarly that has been accessible to me. His exhaustive treatment of all the available evidence has led him to the conclusion that the Hebrew text of the 'Cambridge Document' is not a primary historical document, in the strict sense of the word, but a composition of the twelfth or thirteenth century, based on earlier written material available in Byzantium, partly of a romantic character, itself perhaps based ultimately on oral tradition current in Byzantium. He considers that the purpose

[1] 'An Unknown Khazar Document', *Jewish Quarterly Review*, N.S. 1912, pp. 181 ff. Schechter's article contains photographic facsimiles of the two fragments which constitute the 'Cambridge Document', as well as an edited text and English translation.

[2] 'Beiträge zum Chazarenproblem', *Schriften der Gesellschaft zur Förderung der Wissenschaft des Judentums*, no. 43 (1938). Landau's work has not been accessible to me. I am indebted for this reference to Vernadsky's *Ancient Russia*, p. 212.

of the author was the consolation and encouragement of his fellow Jews suffering hardship or persecution, and that for this purpose he was at pains to recall to their minds the glories of their heroic past. The reading of the name HLGU (Halgo or Helgo), which occurs twice in the document, though not absolutely certain, is virtually established, and Kokovtsov himself appears to entertain no doubt as to his identity with the Oleg of the *Povêst*. He holds, however, that the form of the name HLGU represents the Greek form of the name current in Byzantium in the tenth or eleventh centuries. If this is so the Khazar document must be supposed, like the account of Oleg in the *Povêst*, to represent oral tradition of the Varangian rulers of Kiev current in Greek circles.

There is nothing inherently improbable in this view, though, as Kokovtsov himself points out, no evidence relating to Oleg has, up till the present time, come to light in written Greek sources. We shall see, as we proceed, that stories relating to the events of the period to which the Khazar document has reference were widely current, and have left traces in many Oriental writings, Arabic, Persian and Armenian. We have seen also that the story of Oleg has been enshrined in elaborate saga in Russia. I suspect that it exists in Old Norse saga also; but the evidence for such a view would take too long to establish here. It would be in no way surprising, however, if some saga of the kind postulated by Kokovtsov should have been current in the Greek world at least in the tenth and eleventh centuries. But whatever the source from which the writer of the Khazar document drew his information, we may, while withholding a final judgment on the precise origin and character of the narrative which it contains, regard it as tradition of unique interest relating to a period and milieu which are all too little documented in authentic history.

The text of this so-called 'Cambridge Document' is contained in a fragment of a Hebrew MS. dating from before the close of the thirteenth century, possibly copied from a tenth-century original. The dating is established chiefly on palaeographical grounds.[1] The text relates to the early history of the Khazars, and is especially interesting in view of the extreme sparsity of documents relating to this people.

The Khazars were a Turkish people from the Steppe who formed an important trading state on the Volga, and whose *khagan*, or prince, Bulan, was probably converted to the Jewish religion c. 730, while the conversion of his people may have taken place towards the end of the same century.[2] About the middle of the seventh century the Khazars had subjugated the Bulgars in the neighbourhood of the Sea of Azov, and made the agricultural Slavs in the valleys of the Dnêpr and the Oka tributary to them. Before the end of the century the Crimea was in their hands, and with it the command of the Sea of Azov, and also the steppe between the Volga and the Don—a vantage ground of paramount importance for both strategic and trading interests. During the following centuries they entertained friendly mercantile relations with the Byzantine empire, forming an important buffer state between the Greeks and the Pechenegs on the one hand, and between the Greeks and the Scandinavian state on the Dnêpr on the other. To this end in the ninth century the *khagan*, as the Khazar prince was called, built a new fortified capital at Sarkel[3] near the bend of the Don—a unique stone citadel in a stoneless tract of country, erected by Byzantine engineers.

The document first published by Schechter—the so-called 'Cambridge Document'—relates to the conversion of the Khazars, and also to the relations of the Khazars with their neighbours, notably the king of the Alani, the king of the Turks, the king of the Pechenegs and the king of Macedon (Byzantium).[4] More interesting and important for our purpose is the account which

[1] V. Mošin, 'Les Khazars et les Byzantins', *Byzantion*, Vol. VI (1931), pp. 309 ff. See further *ib. Slavia*, 1938, pp. 191 ff. See, however, Kokovtsov above.
[2] Mošin, *loc. cit.*; cf., however, Vernadsky, *op. cit.* p. 292.
[3] This stone edifice was far-famed as the only stone structure in the area. The name means 'yellow abode'. Cf. also p. 6 above.
[4] See Kokovtsov, *op. cit.*, p. 117, note 1.

the document contains of their relations with Tmutorakan[1] and the kingdom on the Dnêpr, notably the attack made by the Russians against the Khazars about the beginning of the tenth century (perhaps between 907 and 943). According to the Khazar document the leader of the Russians was a certain 'king of Russia', whose name, which occurs twice, is generally read as Halgo or Helgo.[2] This attack is represented in the Khazar document in question as a victory for the Khazars; but the expedition is generally (though not invariably) regarded by modern historians as a part of a great campaign made by Oleg against Byzantium, which the *Povêst* claims as a great victory for the Russians. Greek historians, as we have seen, are silent on the matter, with the exception of a possible reference to Oleg's treaty, to be considered later.

Briefly stated the Khazar document gives the following account of what happened. The Greek emperor Romanus (r. 919–944), who is referred to in the document as 'impious', having incurred the hostility of the Khazar king Joseph by his persecution of the Jews, persuaded the king of Russia, whose name seems to be Halgo or Helgo, to retaliate on the Khazars. 'Helgo' made a night attack on the people of Tmutorakan in the absence of their commander Pesah[3] (Bulshazi), who, on his part, retaliated by attacking the cities of Romanus, and then marched against 'Shorshu'. The text is full of gaps, but we are told that 'when he marched against Shorshu, there their citizens came out of the earth like worms', and that these citizens were conquered from both Russians and Greeks, and were made tributary to the Khazars. Pesah then attacked and conquered Helgu directly, and forced him to attack Byzantium, against which he is here said to have fought four months by sea. He was eventually overcome

---

[1] *Ib.* p. 118, note 4. Schechter read this word differently, and interpreted it as referring to the Severians. See *Povêst*, s.a. 884.

[2] Kokovtsov, *op. cit.* p. 118, note 2.

[3] A comparatively modern Hebrew name. See Kokovtsov, *op. cit.* p. 119, note 8. On the name, or title, Bulshazi, see Kokovtsov, *op. cit.* p. 118, note 6.

by 'Greek fire', and being ashamed to return to his land, 'he went to Persia by sea and fell there'.

For our present purpose the principal interest in this narrative lies in the name of the Russian king. If this is indeed Helgu, as seems practically certain, the point is one of especial importance, since this form of the name is very much nearer to the Scandinavian form Helgi than is the usual Russian form Oleg, and the Khazar document perhaps offers an earlier and more direct testimony to the existence of a Norse prince Oleg than does the *Povêst*. Unfortunately the authenticity of the document is not yet absolutely established, and moreover the actual condition of the document also makes it difficult to identify the course of events or the names with any degree of certainty in their Hebrew guise.[1] Finally, we must bear in mind Kokovtsov's suggestion that the Khazar document is based ultimately on oral tradition current in Byzantium.

The attack of Pesah on the Greek cities, where 'the people came out of the earth like worms', refers almost certainly to the caves of the Crimea and neighbourhood, which already in the eighth century were occupied by Greek monks,[2] and which, though once Khazar territory, had been cut off and included once more in the Greek world. The name of the place *Shorshu*, captured as the final prize by Pesah, is certainly Kherson;[3] for although our document speaks of Atel (Itil) as the Khazar capital, this refers, not to the writer's own time, but to the glorious past which he has been recording. This identification implies that the events referred to above took place at a time when the Khazars had already expanded westwards, after the downfall of the Bulgarian kingdom in the seventh century. Their presence in this neighbourhood in the middle of the ninth century is implied by the *Povêst*, which

[1] Kokovtsov regards the name *Halgo* or *Helgo* as representing a Greek form of the name current in Byzantium in oral form (see above); *op. cit.* pp. xxxivf.

[2] See Vasiliev, *The Goths in the Crimea* (Cambridge, Mass. 1936), p. 89; cf. *ib.* p. 51.

[3] See Kokovtsov, *op. cit.* p. 119, note 9.

refers[1] to them as imposing tribute on the Polians, the 'people of
the plains', and more especially the inhabitants of the district
around Kiev.

I see no reason to doubt the testimony of the *Povêst* in this
matter, and I am inclined to believe that the Khazars, who seem
to be spoken of as in alliance with Tmutorakan,[2] are stationed,
not at Itil, but at Sarkel, in view of a passage in the Khazar
document referring to their conversion. Here we are told that
while the Greeks, Arabs and Jews were contending before the
princes of Khazaria in their efforts to convert them, 'the princes
of Khazaria said: "Behold, there is a cave in the valley of Tizul.
Bring forth for us the books which are there and explain them
to us." And they did so, we are told, and went into the cave. 'And
behold there were there books of the Law of Moses.' It is difficult
to avoid the conclusion that we have here a reference to a library
or book store of one of the rock-built or 'cave' churches of the
Greek monks which had been established in the eighth century.
We may compare the chamber or cupboard in the rock behind
the Buddhist shrine of Tun Hwang in which Sir Aurel Stein
discovered so many of his most precious MSS.

It is tempting to see in the Khazar account of Helgu's expedition against the Khazars and Pesah's reprisals the Khazar version
of two short annals in the *Povêst* (s.a. 6392, 6393; A.D. 884, 885),
according to which Oleg attacked and conquered the stronghold
of Tmutorakan and imposed a light tribute on its people, and
forbade them to pay tribute to the Khazars because they were his
enemies. The fact that Oleg is here represented as victorious may
be accounted for partly on the ground of his initial success, which
is also recognised by the Khazar document,[3] and partly on the
grounds of the natural bias of the Russian chronicler and the later

---

[1] S.a. 6367 (A.D. 859).

[2] See Kokovtsov, *op. cit.* p. 118, note 4, and the references there cited.

[3] It is noteworthy that there is no reference to King Joseph's victory
over Helgo in the Khazar document; but the omission is perhaps more
significant of the medium in which the document was composed than of
historical fact.

and more legendary character of his narrative. The details of the *Povêst*, the 'silken sails', and the palls, gold, wine, etc. which Oleg is represented as taking back with him, indicate the source of this narrative as panegyric poetry, closely akin to Norse skaldic verse, which it closely resembles.[1] It is also interesting to note that at this point[2] the chronicler enters the note that 'the people called Oleg *Vêshchi*, "the Wise", "the Prophetic", or "the Sage", "the Soothsayer"', which suggests that he may have wished to copy the Greek emperor of the time, Leo VI, who was also known as 'the Wise'. We shall see later that exactly the same procedure is followed by Yaroslav after his defeat by the Greeks.

It must not be overlooked that there is a chronological difficulty in identifying the events just discussed with those already referred to in the Khazar document. According to the *Povêst* Oleg's expedition against the Greeks took place in 904. An attack on the Severians is mentioned in the same year before the expedition against the Greeks; but the expeditions against the Severians referred to above took place in 884. We must suppose, therefore, either that more than one attack on the Severians was made by Oleg, or else that the chronology of Oleg's reign is confused in the *Povêst* itself. In any case the dates are difficult to reconcile with the Khazar document, according to which these events took place in 943, during the reign of Romanus in Byzantium, which would be in the time, not of Oleg, but of his ward Igor, while, as we have seen, Greek writers make no direct mention of Oleg's expedition.[3] Such chronological discrepancies are, however, not rare in early records, and I am less inclined to

---

[1] We may refer especially to the poem known as the *Haraldskvaethi*, in which the treasures to be found at the court of King Harold the Fair-haired are enumerated, and include 'splendid swords, girls from the East, cloaks of scarlet with magnificent borders, coats of woven mail, gilded baldrics, engraved helmets and bracelets'. The *Haraldskvaethi* is translated by Kershaw, *Anglo-Saxon and Norse Poems* (Cambridge, 1922), pp. 76 ff.

[2] S.a. 6412–6415 (A.D. 904–907).

[3] Runciman regards Oleg's invasion of Byzantium as 'almost certainly apocryphal'. See *The Emperor Romanus Lecapenus and his Reign* (Cambridge, 1929), p. 36, footnote 2, and also p. 110.

take the Russian chronology *au pied de la lettre* in view of the fact that the form of the name *Helgu* in the Khazar document is much earlier, or at least much nearer to the Norse form Helgi, than the Russian Oleg, which has suffered considerable modification in oral tradition.

My own suggestion as regards this chronological difficulty is this. Oleg is first mentioned in the *Povêst* s.a. 6378–6387 (A.D. 870–879), when we are told that he became the 'fosterer' of Rurik's son Igor. Evidently the exact dates were not known to the chronicler. His death is entered s.a. 6420 (A.D. 912), rather more than thirty years later. Now according to Greek sources, an expedition was made against Byzantium in 941, in the time of Romanus, by Igor. Liudprand of Cremona describes the expedition of Igor, 'king of the Nordmanni', as follows:

'These people had a king named Igor who got together a fleet of a thousand ships or more and sailed for Constantinople. The Emperor Romanus, hearing of this, was distracted by various thoughts; for his naval forces were either engaged against the Saracens or occupied in guarding the islands. He spent some sleepless nights in reflection while Igor devastated the coastlands, and at last he was informed that there were fifteen old battered galleys in the yards which had been allowed to go out of commission. Thereupon he called the ships' carpenters into his presence and said to them:

'"Make haste and get the old galleys ready for service without delay. Moreover, put the fire throwers not only at the bows but at the stern and both sides as well."

'When the galleys had been equipped according to his instructions, he called his most skilful sailors, and bade them give King Igor battle. So they set out; and when King Igor saw them on the open sea he ordered his men to capture them alive and not kill them.... But the merciful and compassionate Lord...lulled the winds and calmed the waves; for otherwise the Greeks would have had difficulty in hurling their fire. As they lay, surrounded by the enemy, the Greeks began to fling their fire all around; and the Rusi, seeing the flames, threw themselves in haste from their ships, preparing to be drowned in the water rather than burned alive in their fire. Some sank to the bottom under the weight of their cuirasses and helmets which they were never to see again; some caught fire even among the billows; not a man escaped save those who managed to reach the shore. For the Rus ships, by reason of their small size, can move in very shallow water where the Greek galleys, because of their greater draught, cannot pass. As the result of this Igor returned to his own country completely demoralised, while the victorious Greeks returned in triumph to Constantinople, bringing a host of prisoners with them. These were all beheaded in the presence of King Hugh's envoy, namely my stepfather, by order of Romanus.'[1]

Now if the chronology of the *Povêst* could be trusted,[2] Igor would already have been a man of some sixty-five years of age, or even more, when he undertook this expedition, and nearly eighty when he undertook his fatal expedition among the Drevlians—a thing not very likely in itself. In all probability the chronology of Oleg's life is confused in Russian sources, which are certainly dependent in general for this period on oral tradition. It is to be suspected that Igor's expedition was even made during the lifetime of his 'fosterer' Oleg, and with his assistance. The account of Oleg's reign is the earliest personal saga contained in the *Povêst*, and its dates are admittedly vague. We have seen that several of the most important events which are attributed to Oleg duplicate those attributed to Igor, whose chronology can be checked from Greek sources. Is it not possible that the chronicler, working on oral traditions, has made two narratives of what was originally a single piece of history?

My own suspicion is that the expeditions were probably undertaken and organised jointly by Igor and Oleg, and that the Russian chronicler has made use of what were originally two variant versions of a single event, or series of events, to form two periods of history running consecutively, pushing the period of

[1] *Antapodosis*, v, ch. xvi (translated by F. A. Wright, London, 1930).
[2] The chronology of Igor's reign is, however, generally admitted to be difficult to accept.

Oleg farther back, either inadvertently, or in order to reconcile variant traditions, or again in order to lengthen the period of Russian history. Some such explanation seems to be justified by the facts; and the process is one with which every student of oral tradition is perfectly familiar. If we accept this suggestion, and bring the upper limit of the chronology of the early years of Oleg and Igor to a later date, the chronology of Igor's life would become in every way more convincing.

The occurrence of the name Helgu in the Khazar document does not, of course, necessarily mean that this Helgu is the Helgi of the *Povêst*,[1] though the Khazar document would seem to point to an attack by the Russians on the Khazars in the time of the Greek emperor Romanus.[2] Now the description of the expedition given in the Khazar document, and the conclusion that the leader, whether Helgu or another, died in Persia, make it extremely probable that this expedition is the one described by the contemporary Arabic writer Mas'udi.[3] According to his narrative,[4] some time not long after Hej. 300 (A.D. 912) about five hundred 'Russian'[5] ships asked and obtained permission from the Khazarian 'king' to enter the 'Khazar River' (the Volga), and so make their way to the 'Khazar Sea' (the Caspian), promising him half the booty which they should obtain from the inhabitants of these regions. Having obtained the permission of this 'prince', they made their way by water to Amol at the mouth of the river Harhaz, and so spread over the Caspian. Detachments of cavalry

---

[1] Mošin, 'Du Nouveau sur le document khazar récemment découvert', *Publications de la Société archéologique russe du royaume des Serbes, Croates, et Slovènes* (Yugoslavia), Vol. 1 (1927), pp. 41 ff.

[2] Crowned 919; ruled till 944.

[3] †c. 943. S. Runciman, *op. cit.* p. 111, footnote 2, places the event soon after 912.

[4] Maçoudi, *Les Prairies d'Or* (Arabic text with French transl. by Barbier de Maynard and Pavet de Courteille), Vol. II (Paris, 1863), pp. 18 ff.

[5] Under the generic name of *Russes* (روس ال) a multitude of peoples are comprised; the most numerous, called الارذمانيون (i.e. *al Nordmān*—,'Norsemen'; see Minorsky, *Encyclopaedia of Islām*, s.v. *Rus*), are said to carry on trade with Spain, Rome, Constantinople (Mas'udi, *loc. cit.* p. 18).

attacked various provinces in the neighbourhood of Barda'a, overran Baku, and ravaged the province of Ardebil, a dependency of Azarbaijan, which is described by Mas'udi as three days' journey from the sea. Their course was marked by great cruelty and bloodshed; women and children were carried away into slavery, while fire and ruin and pillage were carried in every direction among these peaceable people, unused to attack from the sea. On their return they made their way to the islands in the Caspian, where they were attacked by the king of Shirvan, the province in which Baku is situated; but the Russians were completely victorious, and thousands of the Moslems are said to have been slain or drowned. After this success the Russians are said to have given themselves up for some months to piracy, till at last, gorged with booty, they returned to the mouth of the river and sent to the Khazar king the part of the spoil which they had promised to give him. Meanwhile the Moslem subjects of the Khazars brought pressure to bear on him to allow them to take vengeance for their sufferings. Being unable to prevent them, he warned the Russians of the imminent attack; but a large Moslem force, consisting of some fifteen thousand men, well horsed and equipped, and even including a number of Christians from Amol, descended the river to cut off the Russian retreat. The Russians left their ships on seeing them, and a battle took place which lasted three days; but the Moslems were wholly victorious. The Russians perished by the sword, or were drowned. About five thousand escaped, and made their way by land, some to the neighbourhood of Bardas,[1] some to the Bulgars, only to perish by the sword. It is said that nearly thirty thousand perished on the banks of the Khazar river, and Mas'udi winds up his narrative by stating that the Russians never again undertook so hazardous an enterprise. His account is particularly valuable because it is contemporary evidence, for during his lifetime he visited the shores of the Caspian, and the part of his work in which our narrative occurs is regarded as a very reliable authority. We are not, however, wholly dependent on Mas'udi's

[1] I.e. Barda'a.

authority for our knowledge of the Russian attack on Barda'a.
It is clear from references in other early geographers that the
fact of the expedition was widely known. Mas'udi's account is,
indeed, so far as I am aware, the only one which follows the expedition to the final débâcle; but a still fuller and more detailed
account of the earlier parts of the expedition is given by Ibn
Miskawaih,[1] who is stated to have died c. Hej. 421 (A.D. 1043).[2]
His account is exceptionally full and vivid, and of absorbing
interest. It makes on the reader all the impression of being the
account of an eyewitness, and indeed the Arabic writer refers
more than once to his informants who were present at the scenes
so minutely described. Probably nowhere else can be found such
a circumstantial account of the exact procedure of the Norsemen
on taking possession of an important stronghold, such as Barda'a,
whose ruler, here called Marzubān,[3] is said to have been supreme
throughout Azarbaijan.[4] Both this procedure, and indeed the
entire enterprise as we see it in the pages of Ibn Miskawaih, and
also in the less detailed but more complete account of the expedition given by Mas'udi, leave no room to doubt that this
visit of the Russians to the Caspian was not in fact a raid but an
invasion, made with the intention of permanent settlement, such
as the Great Invasion of the Danes and Norsemen in England
in 866.

Ibn Miskawaih tells us many interesting details of the 'Rus'

[1] See Appendix, pp. 135 ff. below.
[2] See the *Tajārib Al-Umam*, by Ibn Miskawaih, ed. by L. Cetani (London,
1909), Vol. I, p. xvii. For an account of Ibn Miskawaih, see the *Encyclopaedia
of Islām*, s.v. and the references there cited.
[3] The word *Marzubān* must originally have been a title and means 'the
warden of the marches'; but it appears in the regnal lists as the name of this
ruler, and is evidently the only one under which he is recorded, and has
reference to his sphere on the western limit of Persian territory. For the
genealogy of this ruler see C. Huart, 'Les Mosāfirides de l'Adherbaïdjân',
in *A Volume of Oriental Studies presented to E. G. Browne* (ed. by Arnold and
Nicholson, Cambridge, 1922), p. 228. The dynasty to which he belonged
was Dailamite. For a full account of Marzubān, see Minorsky's article,
'Musafirids', in the *Encyclopaedia of Islām*.
[4] *The Eclipse*, Vol. v (English transl. Vol. II), p. 68, footnote 1.

which are worth noting. He tells us, for instance, of an epidemic
which is said to have attacked them through indulging excessively
in the fruit 'of which there are numerous sorts there', because,
adds the writer, 'theirs [i.e. that of the "Rus"] is an exceedingly
cold country, where no tree grows, and the little fruit which they
have is imported from distant regions'. Marzubān, we are told,
took advantage of the ravages of this epidemic in the enemy camp
to make an attack, aided by a part of his forces which lay in
ambush, and fell upon the 'Rus' in the rear, killing seven hundred
of them, including their leader. The 'Rus' fought on foot, but
their leader is said to have been mounted on an ass—a most
curious detail for which no comment or explanation is given,
and which is, so far as I know, unique in Varangian annals. It
would perhaps be fanciful to suppose that the 'Rus' leader had,
like the Norse hero Örvar-Oddr and the Russian Oleg (cf. pp. 26 ff.
above), eschewed the use of his horse; but the detail is arresting.
It may be added in this connection that the story of the fruits and
their fatal effects is strikingly reminiscent of the story of the
mythical Scandinavian king, Guthmundr of Glasisvellir, found
in many Norse sagas and in the Danish History of Saxo Grammaticus, according to which those who visited Guthmundr's
garden, of which he was justly proud, and those who ate of his
fruits, were never able to return to their own country.

The epidemic, we are told, continued to grow, and to this
circumstance we owe some interesting details of the 'Rus'
method of burial, and of the behaviour of their enemies in regard
to their tombs, for Ibn Miskawaih adds: 'When one of them died,
they buried with him his arms, clothes, and equipment, and his
wife or some other of his women folk, and his slave, if he happened to be attached to him; this being their practice. After
their power had come to an end, the Moslems disturbed their
graves, and brought out a number of swords which are in great
demand to this day for their sharpness and excellence.'

We are reminded of the Old Norse story of the visit of the
girl Hervör to the tomb of her father Angantýr in order to secure
the sword of her father, as this is related in the *Hervarar Saga*, and

also of the fame which attached to this sword for many generations because it had the reputation of being the death of a man every time it was drawn. The detail noted of the burial of the wife with her husband also not only recalls the narrative of Ibn Faḍlān of the death of the girl with the dead man in the 'Rus' ship burial on the Volga, but is also to be taken in connection with a number of other references in the Norse sagas which suggest the practice of suttee at some period, at any rate in the Swedish royal family (cf. p. 31 above). Finally, it may be pointed out that the mention in Ibn Miskawaih's narrative of the death of the slave with his master is particularly striking in view of the numerous instances which occur in the Norse sagas of two men being buried together, in some cases the second being certainly a slave of the first. I have dealt with these subjects at some length in my forthcoming book on Early Norse religious tradition.

An account of the same raid is also given by Ibn Athir.[1] This account differs only in inconsiderable details from that of Ibn Miskawaih, though it is much shorter than the latter, and it is thought to have little independent value. On the other hand, an independent and important notice of the same raid has also been preserved by the Armenian historian Moses of Kalankatuk, who is said[2] to have come from a village of Kalankatuk in the province of Uti, known to Classical writers as Albania, in the eastern Caucasus. The village is said to be identical with the modern Tarounkatal or Varounkatal. It was near the old 'metropolis' Partav, which is represented by the modern Tertersk on our maps, and which is identical with the village of Barda'a, the

---

[1] For the text of Ibn Athir's work, see Dorn, *Caspia* (St Petersburg, 1875), p. 296. A translation of this part of Ibn Athir's work is given by C. Huart in *A Volume of Oriental Studies presented to E. G. Browne, ed. cit.*, pp. 228 ff.

[2] See Zarbhanalean, *Haikakan Hin Dproutiun* ('Literary History of Ancient Armenia' from the fourth to the thirteenth centuries), pp. 442 ff. (in Armenian). Zarbhanalean refers to a Paris edition of 1860 by Shahnazarean Karapet, who calls Moses *Kalankaytouatsi*. Russian editions have also been published by Emin (Moscow, 1860), and K. Patkanean published a Russian translation: *History of the Albanians* (St Petersburg, 1861).

capital of the province of 'Albania' which preserves the name. This is situated on the Terter, a small tributary of the river Kur, which enters the Caspian between Baku and Lenkoran. Moses is said to have lived in the latter part of the tenth century; and as the chapter in which he deals with the invasion of Albania or Uti by the Ruzik refers immediately before our passage to the death of King Sembat the Martyr which occurred in 914, the work has all the value of an almost contemporary document. It was, moreover, written by an inhabitant of the locality in which the raid took place.

The passage from Moses in which we are interested is as follows: 'After the passage of these periods of time, the Arab people was exhausted, and another people appeared whom they call *Delemenk* ("Dailamites"), from whom came a certain chief, by name Salar; and extending their sway widely, they ruled the Albanians, Persians and Armenians. And coming to Partav, they appropriated that straightway. At the same time there was distributed [1] from the regions of the North a certain people of a different appearance, of foreign type, whom they call *Ruzik*, who in no more than three (?) days like a tempest along the vast sea of the East, the Caspian, suddenly reached the metropolis of the Albanians, Partav, which city, not having the means to resist them, was delivered to the edge of the sword. They made free with all the organisations of the inhabitants. The same Salar himself having surrounded them could not destroy them because they were invincible in strength. But the women of the city, knowing the method, made the Ruz drink a cup of death, who, understanding the deceit, without pity cut down the women and their children. And after being in it six months, they left the city desolate and empty. The rest in an unknown way went to their own land with booty of many kinds.' [2]

---

[1] Reading *bashkhi*, the passive of *bashkhem*, 'to distribute'. A possible translation would be 'extended themselves'. The Shahnazarean edition has a variant reading *bakhi*, 'moved'.

[2] I am indebted to Professor Bailey for the translation and details relating to Moses of Kalankatuk.

It will be noticed that Moses gives the name of the leader of the Dailamites as Salar. The name is, of course, in reality the Persian title *salar*, 'general', 'commander', a title which this ruler inherited from his ancestors. His fuller name is said[1] to have been Salar Mūhammād ibn Musafir al-Dailami.' He was the father of the Marzubān mentioned by Ibn Miskawaih, and the founder of a dynasty of eight princes who are said to have ruled in Azarbaijan in the second half of the tenth and the first half of the eleventh century, though it is possible that their rule began somewhat earlier. The fact that both Ibn Miskawaih and Ibn Athir place the 'Rus' raid in the time of Marzubān, while Moses of Kalankatuk places it in the time of his father Salar, is not, in reality, a serious discrepancy, since 'Salar' was displaced during his lifetime by his son Marzubān; and he is stated to have lived in retirement 'in another fortress', and to have been still alive and in touch with his son after the departure of the 'Rus'.

Other early writers also bear witness to the attack of the 'Rus' on Barda'a. Thus in the *Hudūd al-'Álam*,[2] 'The Regions of the World', a Persian gazetteer of various countries as known to the Persian author of the second half of the tenth century, we read of 'Mubaraki, a large village at the gate of Barda'. There the camp of the Russians (*Rusiyān*) stood when they came and seized (*bisitadand*) Barda'.'[3] Other references are cited by Professor Minorsky, the translator of the work. Further, the Persian writer Marvazi,[4] who was a native of Merv and lived in the eleventh century, also states of the 'Rus' that they 'once sailed into the Khazar Sea and became masters of Barda'a for a time', and he adds that their valour and courage were well known, 'so

---

[1] For the particulars given here relating to the Dailamites, see an interesting account of the dynasty in the article by C. Huart referred to above.

[2] Translated and annotated by Professor V. Minorsky (London, 1937), p. 144. The writer of the *Hudūd*, or his source, was especially well informed in regard to tradition relating to the west of the Caspian. See Barthold, Preface to Minorsky's edition, p. 29.

[3] *Hudūd, ed. cit.* p. 144; cf. p. 398.

[4] *Sharaf Al-Zamān Ṭāhir Marvazī*, ed. and transl. by V. Minorsky (London, 1942), p. 118.

that any one of them is equal to a number of any other nation. If they had horses and were riders, they would be a great scourge to mankind.'[1] In the *Tarikhe Ṭabaristán* by Ibn Isfandiyar,[2] which is believed to have been written *c.* 1216, we read as follows:

'This year [A.D. 910] 16 ships filled with Russians[3] came to Ábasgún,[4] as they had already done in the time of Sayyid Ḥasan b. Zayd,[5] who defeated and slew them. This time they wasted and looted Ábasgún and the adjacent coasts, and carried off or slew many Musulmáns. The governor of Sárí, Abu'd-Darghám Aḥmad b. al-Qásim, wrote news of this to Abu'l-'Abbás. Next year the Russians returned in greater force, burned Sarí and Panjáh-hazár, and carried off many prisoners. Then they sailed to Chashma-Rúd in Daylamán; but, while some of them were on land, a number of the people of Gílán descended to the seashore, burned their ships, and slew those who had landed. Shírwánsháh, King of the Khazars, hearing of this, intercepted such of their ships as had escaped and destroyed them and their crews, and thenceforth the marauding raids of the Russians were stopped.'

References to the 'raid' or raids of the 'Rus' on Barda'a occur also in later authors. Thus in the *Syrian Chronicle* of Gregori Abulfaraj,[6] known as Barhebraeus, we read that in the year Hej. 333 (A.D. 944), in which Mustakfi, the son of Muktafi, began to reign, a number of people, including the Alani, the Slavi, and the Lazgi, 'came out and, devastating the land as far as Azarbaijan, destroyed the city of Barda'a, in which they slew twenty thousand men, and then departed'. Again, according to the *Moslem*

[1] *Marvazī, ed. cit.* p. 36.
[2] Abridged translation by E. G. Browne (London, 1905), p. 198.
[3] I.e. 'Rus'.
[4] An important port on the south-east shores of the Caspian.
[5] Fl. c. 863.
[6] Abulfaraj was also called Barhebraeus because of his Jewish descent. He was born in Armenia in 1226, and was made bishop of Aleppo at the age of twenty. His Chronicle of universal history in Syriac is among his best known writings.

Annals of Abulfeda,[1] in the year Hej. 332 (A.D. 943), certain
'Rus', 'having left their homes by ship, and having been trans-
ported by way of the Caspian Sea and the River Kur, made their
way to the city of Barda'a, occupied it, and plundered it and put
the inhabitants to the sword, and at length returned home by the
way they had come'. Finally, we may refer to Yaqut,[2] who in his
Geographical Dictionary tells us that the 'Rus' 'savagely oppressed
Barda'a until God drove them away and destroyed them'.[3]

Before leaving the subject of the Oriental traditions of this
'raid', it should be mentioned that some tradition of it which
would seem to be genuine, though admittedly vague, and, of
course, wholly unhistorical in its setting, seems to have formed
the basis of the story of the attack made by the 'Russians' on
Barda'a in the Persian romance of Alexander the Great, known
as the *Iskandar-Nama*,[4] and composed by the Persian poet
Nizami. Nizami was born c. 1140–41 at Ganja, now Kirovabad
(Russian, Elizavetpol), not far from Barda'a, the scene of the
raid, on the River Terter, and the district to which Moses of
Kalankatuk belonged. Nizami would, therefore, be in a
fortunate position to know any traditions about the past history
of this district. It is a curious fact that, unlike the majority of
eastern versions of the Alexander tradition, Nizami introduces

---

[1] Born A.D. 1273 at Damascus; died A.D. 1331. He was a famous Arab
historian and geographer, and from 1310 he ruled over the principality of
Hamal in Syria as an independent ally of the sultan. His *Annals* form one
of the most important sources for the history of the Saracen empire.

[2] Born in Greece in 1179; died in Aleppo in 1229. He was a famous
Arab geographer and biographer. His *Mu'jam ul-Buldan*, 'Geographical
Dictionary', is his greatest work, but he also wrote an important 'Diction-
ary of Learned Men', the *Mu'jam ul-Udabā*.

[3] My references to the works of Abulfaraj, Abulfeda and Yaqut are
taken from F. Erdmann, *De Expeditione Russorum versus Berdaam* (Casani,
1826), Vol. I, pp. 26 ff. For further references, see Dorn, *Caspia*, pp. 285 ff.

[4] Canto LV, v, 21 (English transl. by G. Wilberforce Clarke, 'The
Sikandar Nāma' (London, 1881)). For a study of early versions of the
Alexander legend in the East, see Nöldeke, 'Beiträge zur Geschichte des
Alexanderromans', *Denkschriften der kaiserlichen Akademie der Wissen-
schaften*, Vol. XXXVIII (1890), no. 5.

the story of the raid into his narrative of Alexander's exploits, and even makes it a major incident in his narrative. The association with Alexander is, of course, quite fantastic; but when one turns to the *Iskandar-Nama* after reading Ibn Miskawaih one is struck by the familiarity of certain details which sound like oral reminiscences of a common original, such as the frequent references to the excavation of buried treasure, the carrying off of the women and children, and the pillaging of the town of Barda'a itself; and it is interesting to find the terror of the 'Rus' still looming large in the mind of the poet Nizami, who lived in the neighbourhood of their temporary stronghold at Barda'a, and who has made their overthrow the crowning glory of the greatest conqueror of antiquity.[1]

These and other considerations, which point clearly to the deep impression made by the 'Rus' invasions into the Caspian provinces, make it difficult to doubt that we are dealing with the same attack against the Khazars which is described in the Hebrew document already discussed. The reference to the death of the leader in Persia at the close of the Hebrew document is in striking accordance with the notice of the poisoning incident mentioned by Moses of Kalankatuk, and with the account both of the dysentery suffered by the 'Rus' and also of the tremendous massacre of the 'Rus' at the hands of the Moslems in the great battle which closed the campaign. And here we may recall Mas'udi's words that before the battle the 'Rus' left their ships and went on land, and we may refer to the words of Marvazi: 'If they had horses and were riders, they would be a great scourge to mankind.'

---

[1] Elsewhere also Nizami shows special interest in the 'Rus'. One section of his narrative poem *Heft Peiker* relates to 'a Slav (*Saklab*) princess with ruddy cheeks like fire', who tells a story of a 'Rus' town to the prehistoric Persian king, Bahram Gur. This story looks like a version of the theme of the early Norse poem contained in the Elder Edda, and known as the *Sigrdrífumál*, and of the prose account of the finding of Brynhildr by Sigurthr in the *Völsungasaga*. (See the *Heft Peiker*, edited by Ritter and Rypka, Leipzig, 1934), pp. 178 ff. The work is translated into English by C. E. Wilson (London, 1924), pp. 171 ff.

The attack of the 'Rus' indeed seems to have come perilously near to success. It is clear that the 'Rus' themselves were planning permanent settlement in Barda'a, whatever their intentions farther east. This can be seen as well from their conciliatory policy to the inhabitants as from their local fortifications and elaborate organisation. Their task was undoubtedly greatly facilitated by the local dissensions between the Kurdish and Dailamite chiefs, as well as the family differences among the members of the Dailamite dynasty; and we may assume with great probability that the 'Rus' were kept well informed of the local politics of this highly fertile and wealthy region by the Khazars on the northern shores of the Caspian, who were evidently accessory to the 'raid', and undoubtedly hoped to profit by its successful accomplishment. I am inclined to associate the attempt of the whaler Ohthere to make his way up the northern Dvina, and Wulfstan's eastern voyage to the Æstii in the time of Alfred the Great, with these Viking attempts to occupy the southern Caspian region, probably with a view to opening up trade with Central Asia. It is probable that we shall know more of the inner history of these events when our knowledge of the Khazar state is more fully co-ordinated. In the meantime it is interesting to study in the pages of Ibn Miska-waih the fullest and soberest narrative of the occupation of enemy territory by the Vikings which we possess in any records of these people.

It should, however, be mentioned that opinion has always been considerably divided among scholars as to the number of the 'Rus' invasions of the Caspian, and as to whether Mas'udi is, in reality, reporting a different raid from that described by Ibn Miskawaih and Moses. The *Tarikhe Tabaristán* refers to an earlier raid than either of these. On the other hand the poet Khaqani, who was born, like Nizami himself, in Ganjeh (now Elizavetpol) in Azarbaijan, in 1106–7, in several panegyric poems praises the Shrirvānshāh, the ruler Akhestan, whose capital was at Baku, and who was born in the same year as Khaqani himself, for his destruction of the 'Rus' fleets which had raided to the west and south of the Caspian and occupied an island (probably Sārī) of the southern Caspian, and even established themselves for some time at Shemakha.[1] It is clear, therefore, that we are concerned with a long series of raids and attempts at settlement, and identification is still somewhat hazardous in regard to the raids of the first part of the tenth century. The view most in favour among Orientalists is that three incursions[2] of the Norsemen took place within fifty years:

1. Into Ābaskūn, the port on the south-east of the Caspian, in the time of Hasan Ibn Zeid (A.D. 864–84).

2. Into Ābaskūn, between A.D. 909 and 914 (Mas'udi's raid).

3. On the Island of Sārī and to the area of Pandjāh Hazār or into Dailam, c. A.D. 943–4[3] (Ibn Miskawaih's raid).

But it seems fairly clear to me that the raid described in detail by Moses refers to the early part of the century, c. 914,[4] and that he, like the Tarikhe Ṭabaristán, knew of a still earlier raid. It seems equally clear that Ibn Miskawaih's raid is also identical with that described by Moses.

Before leaving the story of Oleg and the Khazars, a final reference must be made to the manner of his death. We have seen that according to the Hebrew document, the Russian king Helgu, being ashamed to return home after his defeat, went to Persia and died there. It is worth while, in view of this curious statement, to return to the account of the death of Oleg as recorded in the Povêst, even at the cost of some repetition. The entry is made immediately after the treaty of Oleg with the Greeks, which was implemented by Russian envoys, who, during their sojourn in Byzantium, are said to have been instructed in the

---

[1] See Khanykov, Mélanges asiatiques tirés du Bulletin Historico-Philologique de l'Académie...de St. Pétersbourg, Tome III, 1858, pp. 114 ff. See further Dorn, Caspia, p. 240.

[2] Neither Kunik nor Dorn consider that Svyatoslav succeeded in reaching the Caspian in his expedition eastward in 965. See Dorn, Caspia, pp. 301 ff.

[3] See Muḥammad 'Ali Jamālzādeh, Tārīkh i Ravābiṭ i Rūs va Irān (Berlin, 1920–2), where, however, the third raid is dated in 921. See further Minorsky, Encycl. Islām, s.v. Rus.

[4] See Dorn, Caspia, pp. 41, 285 f.

Greek faith. The story probably reflects an early tradition of the beginning of Christianity in Kiev,[1] the religion to be nursed and given royal sanction in the next generation by Olga, who was probably Oleg's own daughter. It is probably in the light of such a tradition of Oleg's pact with the Greeks and the opening of the flood gates of Christianity in heathen Kiev that the peculiar circumstances of Oleg's death are to be explained.

We are told that when autumn came, immediately after these events, Oleg bethought him of his horse, which he had caused to be well fed, but had never mounted. Such a strange and apparently inconsequent entry must have struck even the chronicler himself as requiring further elucidation, for he immediately returns to the beginning of the story which he evidently had in mind in making this entry, and relates it at length. We are told that Oleg had once made enquiry of some *volkhvy*, 'shamans', and *kudesniki*, 'sorcerers', as to the cause of his death, and had been told that from the steed which he loved and which he was riding he should meet his death. Oleg, as we have seen (p. 23 above), immediately decided never again to mount the horse, or to see it again, but nevertheless gave orders that it should be suitably fed and well cared for. 'He thus let several years pass before he attacked the Greeks'; but at a later date he summoned his head groom and enquired about the horse. On being told that it was dead he laughed and mocked the *kudesnik* ('sorcerer') and, ordering a horse to be saddled, he went to inspect the skeleton. Dismounting he laughed and said: 'Shall I get my death from this skull?' And he stamped upon it with his foot. The rest of the story need not detain us here. A serpent crawled out of the skull and bit him so that he died. There can be no doubt that in the

---

[1] The eleventh-century writer Marvazi, who is evidently following Khwarazmian tradition, assigns the beginning of Russian Christianity to Hej. 300 (c. A.D. 923), and though this date is questioned by Minorsky (see the *Sharaf Al-Zamān Ṭāhir Marvazī*, pp. 36, 118), it is certainly more in accordance with the tradition of the early annals of the *Povêst* than the years 988–989, to which date the Conversion is assigned in the actual official entry in the *Povêst* itself.

mind of the chronicler the death of Oleg is directly connected with the contempt which he had shown for the native pre-Christian religion of the country. It is interesting to add that the chronicler immediately adds the story of Apollonius of Tyana in illustration of what may be accomplished through witchcraft and enchantment, and that the first accomplishments here related of the saint, evidently suggested by the story of Oleg, are his ability to tame wild horses, and to banish serpents and scorpions.

It will be seen that the account of the death of Oleg is very much in the nature of saga, and cannot for a moment be treated as a serious account of what actually took place. Moreover, we have seen that the account is closely related to the account of the death of the Norse saga hero Örvar-Oddr, and that both stories have their origin in a common theme derived very possibly from Turkish sources (cf. p. 26 above). For this reason I cannot agree with Mošin in regarding the account of Oleg's death in the *Povêst* as any serious argument against identifying him with the Helgu of the Khazar document. The conclusion to which the evidence of the *Povêst* seems to me to point is that the exact nature or whereabouts of the death of Oleg was not clearly remembered in Russian tradition, and therefore a foreign story has been substituted for it. Such a process generally takes place in oral tradition, however, when some vague memory of the original story finds an answering echo in the new story which is substituted for it. The two outstanding features of the death of Oleg in the Russian tradition—his association with his horse, and his death from the bite of an adder—probably therefore echo something in the original story. In traditional oral Russian poetry the Turkish nomad enemies are invariably pictured as dragons or serpents, and the conception is as old as Herodotus. We have seen that the leader of the 'Rus' is said by the Arabic writer Ibn Miskawaih to have been mounted on an ass—a sufficiently re-markable thing in itself. It is possible, therefore, that the story of the death of Oleg in the *Povêst* may reflect some memories of his death in the east in fighting against a Turkish people, and also the fact that he had no horse. I should not for a moment be inclined to press this suggestion; but I have thought it worth while to make it in order to show that the statement of the *Povêst* that Oleg died in Russia, and the date under which his death is entered, cannot be taken as serious evidence for either the time, or place, or manner of the death of the hero, though undoubtedly some germ of genuine tradition underlies the entries of the Russian chronicle even for this early hero, in what is perhaps the most legendary part of this chronicle.

CHAPTER IV

VLADIMIR I

When we compare the account of the reign of Vladimir I with that of his predecessors, we are struck at once by the scarcity of personal reminiscences of a heroic character, and of incidents which suggest the existence of the background of heroic poetry, whether narrative or panegyric. It has sometimes been suggested that such poetry may have given rise to certain anecdotes contained in the *Povêst*, which appear to be based on oral tradition. We may refer to the story (s.a. 6500, A.D. 992) which relates to a single combat between a youth of Kiev and a Pecheneg champion. The story tells how the Pechenegs sent a message to Vladimir to challenge a hero of his court to encounter one of their champions in single combat. None of the heroes of his court dared to undertake the exploit till at last an old man came forward and offered his young son, who, though of no great size, is said to have possessed extraordinary strength. The Pecheneg champion was of gigantic stature, but the youth encountered and overcame him in open combat between the two armies.

The motif is a common one in folk tales, but it also bears a close resemblance to an episode in the Icelandic saga of Björn Hítdoelakappi,[1] which is said to have taken place during Björn's sojourn in Russia at the court of Valdimarr (i.e. Vladimir I). The story relates how Björn challenged and overcame a certain Kaldimarr, a near relative of Valdimarr himself.[2] The story as related in the *Povêst* bears all the marks of oral tradition.

A somewhat more sophisticated story, which is also in all probability based on oral tradition, relates how on one occasion, as the *boyars* were feasting with the prince, they began to grumble

---

[1] *Bjarnar Saga Hítdoelakappa* (ed. Ásmundarson, Reykjavík, 1898), pp. 9 f.

[2] For a discussion of the relationship between the Russian and the Norse stories, see F. Braun, *loc. cit.* pp. 172 ff.

because they had to eat their food with wooden spoons, where-upon Vladimir supplied them with spoons of silver, remarking that with such a *druzhina* he could win plenty of such wealth, but he could not with wealth obtain such another *druzhina*. From this and other anecdotes in the *Povêst* we can be in no doubt that popular stories were current in later times relating to the period of Vladimir I. But the nature of the stories—the element of wit and sophistication in the story of the spoons, and the democratic atmosphere of the story of the champion—points to saga rather than to heroic poetry as the more probable medium of transmission. The existence of the story in the saga of Björn may perhaps be held to confirm this view.

This democratic atmosphere is in sharp contrast to that of another story which is otherwise comparable with that of the Pecheneg champion, and which relates to a single combat between Mstislav of Tmutorakan and Rededya, a mighty Kasog champion. This story is related in the *Povêst* s.a. 6530 (A.D. 1022), and refers, of course, to a later period than that of which we have just made mention. It relates to the warfare between Yaroslav the Wise and Mstislav, who opposed him with a mixed force of Khazars and Kasogs. It is very probable that this story is not wholly independent of that related under the reign of Vladimir I, but the later story is distinctly aristocratic in atmosphere, and heroic in tone, and has probably been transmitted through the medium of heroic poetry.

According to the *Povêst* (s.a. 6478, A.D. 970), Vladimir I was the son of Svyatoslav, Olga's son, and of a certain Malyusha, the daughter of Mal, prince of the Drevlians, the forest people to the west of Kiev. It is commonly stated in modern Russian histories that Vladimir's mother was a slave woman;[1] but there is nothing in the text to suggest this. Malyusha's father was a prince, and though she herself was undoubtedly at the court of Olga in some

[1] The idea has doubtless gained wide currency owing to the gibe of Rogned (Ragnheithr), who, when asked in marriage by Vladimir, replied: 'I do not want to pull off the boots of a slave's son' (*ne khoshchyu razut robichishcha*), s.a. 6488 (A.D. 980).

kind of inferior or official capacity, probably as stewardess or bursar,[1] her position was doubtless an honourable and highly responsible one. Moreover as the sister of Dobrynya, Vladimir's *voevoda* in Novgorod, she would probably be held in high esteem. For the author of the *Povêst*, with his Greek education and city life, the Drevlians are backwoodsmen, and as a forest people they no doubt retained conservative and even barbaric customs and standards. But their relations with Igor and Olga, and the subsequent careers of Dobrynya and of Dobrynya's son Constantine (see p. 99 below), make it clear that their royal family played an important part in Russian politics. Indeed Malyusha's position at Olga's court would seem to strengthen the impression which we get from the relations of the Drevlian princely family with that of Igor and his sons that the Scandinavian princes were really dependent on a settled Slavonic order of things which they left for the most part undisturbed, much as the members of our modern ephemeral governments rely on the permanent secretaries for the actual execution of state business. We shall see as we proceed that this impression of the *voevodas* as the really stable element in the early body politic of Russia is greatly strengthened by a study of the part which they play under Vladimir's successors.

According to the *Povêst*, Vladimir I first comes into prominence as ruler of Novgorod. He is said to have owed his rule there to the invitation of his uncle Dobrynya, himself a Slav, and more exactly a Drevlian. Dobrynya in consequence was afterwards created, or more probably reinstated, as *voevoda* of the city by Vladimir himself. Moreover, according to the same source, Vladimir became ruler in Kiev at a later date, not in virtue of his descent, which is represented as half Slav, but as the result of the treachery and intrigue of Yaropolk's Slavonic *voevoda* Blud. This insistence on the dependence of the royal line on Slavonic 'king makers', as we may call Dobrynya and Blud, and the break with

[1] She is stated in the *Povêst* to have been Olga's *klyuchnitsa*, which is generally translated 'house-keeper', or 'confidante', but which is probably to be interpreted as something in the nature of a confidential stewardess.

the direct Scandinavian tradition which is postulated by the chronicler with the accession of Vladimir I, are by no means accidental. They are part of a definite ideal which the chronicler has set before himself—the ideal of demonstrating the continuity of Slavonic culture, the unessential and impermanent character of the Scandinavian occupation, the origin of Russian Christianity and culture with the first Slavonic ruler Vladimir I, its consolidation under his successors, till the final emergence of a united Russian nation under his great descendant, Vladimir Monomakh.

The account of the reign of Vladimir I is mainly occupied with his campaigns against the surrounding tribes, and with his conversion to Christianity. His campaigns follow a definite plan, and are a carefully thought-out scheme of consolidation, beginning with the Varangians in Kiev itself, and passing first to the neighbouring Slavonic and Lithuanian tribes, such as the Lyakhs, the Vyatichians, and the Yatvings and Radimichians in the north, whom, being for the most part forest peoples, he overcame without much difficulty. With the Bulgarians he was fain to make peace; but a campaign against Kherson was completely successful.[1] It is noteworthy that here, as in most of his earlier conquests, his success was brought about by treachery in the camp of his enemies.

The frequency with which such 'diplomatic' successes are attributed to him conveys the impression that he was more of a statesman than a general; and this impression is confirmed by the

[1] For a valuable discussion of Vladimir's expedition to Kherson, see Vasiliev, *The Goths in the Crimea* (Cambridge, Mass. 1936), pp. 132 ff., and the references there cited. An account of the invasion of the Crimea in the early years of the ninth century is attributed in an Old Russian version of the Life of St Stephen of Surozh to a certain Russian prince Bravlin. Some Russian scholars hold that this Bravlin is no other than St Vladimir himself, and place this episode in the life of St Stephen of Surozh in the tenth century (see Vasiliev, *op. cit.* p. 111). Is it possible that the name Bravlin is a corrupt form of *Murovlenín*, the old form of the surname of Ilya Muromets, who is elsewhere associated with St Vladimir, and who, in the *byliny*, fulfils functions which bear some resemblance to those of the *voevoda* of the early princes of Kiev? For an alternative suggestion, see Vernadsky, *Ancient Russia*, pp. 280 f.

account of the foreign embassies which are represented as coming to his court from the surrounding nations, and as endeavouring to persuade him to adopt their faith, notably the Mohammedan Bulgars, the Catholic Germans, the Jewish Khazars, and finally the Byzantine Greeks. Moreover the king is also represented as sending his own envoys among these peoples to make personal enquiries as to their religious practices. Taken on its face value we should judge from this that a tradition was current regarding the lively intercourse between Kiev and the surrounding nations at this period[1]—an intercourse which would necessarily carry with it lively trade relations, and which would naturally follow from such relations. There can indeed be no doubt that Vladimir's military and diplomatic activities all suggest the consolidation of a state which, though still small, was gradually coming to take its place among the nations of eastern Europe.

It would be interesting to know exactly how much value we can safely attach to Vladimir's religious researches. The Khazar document referred to above contains a passage very similar to the story of the various religious missions sent to Vladimir's court in the *Povêst*. This story relates that representatives of the Greeks, the Arabs, and the Jews, came to plead the cause of their religions before the Khazar princes. In this case the Jews prevailed; for the king, we are told, ordered books to be brought from a 'cave', and on receiving them he found that they contained the Books of the Law of Moses, which commended itself to him.[2] It is to be suspected that the 'cave' in question is one of the rock-built churches founded on the shores of the Black Sea about the eighth century (cf. p. 45 above). The question at once arises: Is the *Povêst* making use of Khazar documents at this point? Or are Russians and Khazars alike making use of a

---

[1] See, e.g., Cedrenus, *Historiarum Compendium*, Vol. II (Bonn, 1839), p. 551.

[2] See Schechter, 'An Unknown Khazar Document', *Jewish Quarterly Review*, N.S. 1912, p. 215. Incidentally we also have record of a mission to the western Turks from the Khalif Hisham (A.D. 724–743) for the purpose of converting them to Islam. The mission was unsuccessful. See Marquart, in *Festschrift für Hirth* (Berlin, 1920), p. 290.

common tradition, possibly Islamic (e.g. Khwarazmian) in origin? It is worth noting that Khwarazm is the district from which the Jews came who carried out the conversion, the districts of the other envoys being Baghdad and 'Greece'. By Greece, of course, Byzantium is indicated.

At this point it is interesting to return to the Khwarazmian tradition cited by the eleventh-century Persian writer Marvazi. This tradition is unknown from other sources, but according to it, the 'Rus'[1] had become Christians in the year 923; but 'when they entered the fold of Christianity, the faith blunted their swords, the door of their livelihood was closed to them, they returned to hardships and poverty, and their livelihood shrank. Then they desired to become Muslims, that it might be lawful for them to make raids and holy war, and so make a living by returning to their former practices. They therefore sent messengers to the ruler of Khwarazm, four kinsmen of their king; for they had an independent king called V. lādmīr (Vladimir), just as the king of the Turks is called *khaqan*, and the king of the Bulgars *btltu*. Their messengers came to Khwarazm and delivered their message. The Khwarazm-shah was delighted at their eagerness to become Muslims, and sent someone to teach them the religious laws of Islam. So they were converted.'[2]

The fact that Marvazi knew Vladimir by name makes one inclined to accept his statement, despite the fact that it is unsupported by other early authorities. We know, as I have said above, that Christianity was already well rooted in Kiev long before Vladimir's conversion. Such a lapse as that described by Marvazi would not only help to account for the necessity for an elaborate renewal under Vladimir, such as the *Povêst* relates, but it would also accord well with the anti-Christian attitude of Svyatoslav,

---

[1] 'The Rus', says Marvazi, 'live on an island in the sea.' He is doubtless translating the Norse name for Novgorod and Russia in general, *Holmgarthr*, *holm* being Old Norse for a flat island, such as that on which Novgorod stands. It is clear, therefore, that his narrative has reference to the Norsemen. See *Marvazī, ed. cit.* p. 36.

[2] *Marvazī, ed. cit.* p. 36.

who, when urged by Olga to accept Christianity, spurned the idea, declaring that his *druzhina* would scorn him if he were a Christian.[1] We need not accept *au pied de la lettre* Marvazi's statement that the conversion to Islam actually took place under Vladimir; but the embassy which Marvazi describes may well correspond to the preliminary mission which Vladimir is stated in the *Povêst* to have sent to the Bulgars. Barthold observes[2] pertinently that there is nothing improbable in itself in Marvazi's statement that Vladimir's envoys went to Khwarazm, since the Bulgars themselves sought religious instruction there.

The question has been raised as to whether Russia was at any time a vassal state of Byzantium, and, if so, at what period it became a subject state. Vasiliev points out[3] that no trade treaties are recorded between the Russians and the Greeks after those of Oleg, Igor and Svyatoslav, and that though both Vladimir and Yaroslav made expeditions against the Greeks, these are not followed by any treaties.[4] Vasiliev is of the opinion[5] that the explanation lies in the fact that when the Byzantine emperor gave the Greek princess Anna, probably his own sister, in marriage to Vladimir I on condition that he became a Christian,[6] and also on condition that he sent auxiliary troops to aid the emperor against the rebellion of Phocas,[7] the emperor also received simultaneously from Vladimir a promise of fealty to the

---

[1] *Povêst*, s.a. 6456–6463 (A.D. 948–955).

[2] See Minorsky, *ed. cit.* p. 119. Barthold's article, 'Arab Sources on Russians', in *Sovetskoye Vostokovedeniye* (ed. by the Academy of Sciences of the U.S.S.R.), Vol. I, 1941, has not been accessible to me.

[3] 'Was Old Russia a Vassal State of Byzantium?' *Speculum*, Vol. VII (1932), pp. 350ff.

[4] Cf. however Cedrenus, Vol. II, p. 351, where lively trade intercourse on equal terms seems to be implied in the reign of Vladimir.

[5] 'Was Old Russia a Vassal State of Byzantium?' *Speculum*, Vol. VII, pp. 350ff.; cf. *History of the Byzantine Empire*, Vol. I (transl. by Mrs Ragozin, Madison, 1928), p. 421.

[6] S.a. 6496 (A.D. 988).

[7] Vasiliev, *loc. cit.* See also S. H. Cross, 'The Earliest Medieval Churches in Kiev', *Speculum*, Vol. XI (1936), p. 479, and the references there cited. We may refer in particular to the following passage: πλοῖα παρασκευάσας

Byzantine ruler himself as overlord. Vasiliev supports this suggestion by pointing to an account written by Michael Psellos, a Greek writer and scholar of the eleventh century, who was an eyewitness of the Russian attack made by Igor on Greece in 1043. His account bears the significant title: περὶ τῆς τῶν Ῥώσων ἐπαναστάσεως ('On the Revolt or Rising of the Rus').[1] Vasiliev, though careful not to give too much weight to the argument, is of the opinion that the use of the word ἐπανάστασις, 'revolt', or 'insurrection', suggests that the Greeks had reason to regard the Russians as their vassals. It may be added that Skylitzes also uses the word κατάρχων, which may be translated *subregulus*.[2]

My own judgment is, on the whole, in accordance with the opinion expressed by Vasiliev; but Professor Cross regards Vladimir as the 'ally and equal of the Byzantine emperors', and considers that the marriage merely confirmed their position.[3] A similar view is expressed by Professor Kadlec.[4] In this matter they seem to be basing their conclusions on the account of the Russians' relations with Byzantium at this period as given by the Arabic chronicler Yahya Ibn Sa'id of Antioch, who wrote in the first half of the eleventh century. His account refers to the rebellion of Phocas Bardas against the Emperor Basil II in 988, and the passage which definitely concerns us is as follows:

'La situation était devenue grave, et l'empereur Basile en était préoccupé à cause de l'avantage qu'il avait sur lui. Les caisses étaient vides. Dans ce besoin pressant (Basile) fut contraint de demander secours au roi des Russes, qui étaient ses ennemis. Le

νυκτὸς καὶ τούτοις ἐμβιβάσας Ῥώς (ἔτυχε γὰρ συμμαχίαν προσκαλεσά-μενος ἐξ αὐτῶν, καὶ κηδεστὴν ποιησάμενος τὸν ἄρχοντα τούτων Βλα-διμηρὸν ἐπὶ τῇ ἑαυτοῦ ἀδελφῇ Ἄννῃ) (Cedrenus, Vol. ii, Bonn, 1839, p. 444).

[1] Michael Psellos, *Chronographie*, Vol. ii (ed. and transl. by É. Renauld, Paris, 1928), pp. 8 ff.

[2] Cedrenus, Vol. ii, p. 551.

[3] 'Medieval Russian Contacts with the West', *Speculum*, Vol. x (1935), p. 139.

[4] *Cambridge Medieval History*, Vol. iv (Cambridge, 1927), p. 209.

(Russe) y acquiesça; après quoi ils firent une alliance de parenté, et le roi des Russes épousa la sœur de l'empereur Basile à la condition qu'il se ferait baptiser avec tout le peuple de son pays. Le grand peuple des Russes n'avait à cette époque aucune loi ni aucune foi religieuse. Par après, l'empereur Basile lui envoya des métropolites et des évêques qui baptisèrent le roi et tout le peuple de son pays; en même temps il lui envoya sa sœur qui fit bâtir plusieurs églises dans le pays des Russes.

'La question du mariage ayant été conclu entre eux, les troupes russes arrivèrent aussi, et après s'être jointes aux troupes Grecs, qui étaient avec l'empereur Basile, se mirent en marche tous ensemble pour attaquer Bardas Phocas par terre et par mer, vers Chrysopolis. (Ces troupes) vainquirent Phocas.'[1]

Vasiliev in an earlier work expresses the view that 'only the intervention of the Russian auxiliary corps sent by Prince Vladimir prevented the fall of the Emperor'.[2]

My own impression is that the important place which Vladimir I holds in Russian history is principally due to his Greek alliance. The Drevlians, owing to their position behind the forests, appeared barbaric to the composer of the *Povêst*, writing in Kiev, where Greek influence was strong. But they were evidently a people of political strength and ability, and the heirs of early Slavonic culture, and it would seem that it was to the support of the Drevlians and the Slavs in the neighbourhood of Kiev that Vladimir owed his throne, so far as we can judge from the records which have come down to us. The Drevlians doubtless made use of him to reduce the influence and power of the Norsemen, first in Novgorod, and later in Kiev. It is, however, to be doubted if he could have acted effectively against the powerful standing garrisons of the Scandinavians without Greek support in some

---

[1] *Histoire de Yahya-Ibn-Sa'id d'Antioche*, ed. and transl. into French by Krachkovsky and Vasiliev, II (*Patrologia Orientalis*, Vol. XXIII, 1932, pp. 423 f.). Cf. also Leo the Deacon, *Historiae*, Vol. x, 9 (Bonn, 1828), pp. 173 f., where again we are told that the Greek fleet made use of τριήρεις πυρφόρους, 'fire-throwing triremes'.

[2] *Speculum*, Vol. VII (1932), pp. 350 ff.

form or other. It may well be that the Emperor Basil was glad of his help in a crisis; but it is difficult to believe that in general a power which had repeatedly defeated its northern neighbours by Greek fire was not in a position to make its own terms with Vladimir.

It is clear from the accounts of the Greek and Arabic historians that the emperor was in need of outside help at the time of Phocas' rebellion, and that the troops sent by Vladimir I supplied that need. But the nature of the relations—the foundation of a Christian Church in Kiev, and the royal marriage—suggests that a more permanent bond was contemplated. I have no hesitation in suggesting that the real object of the Greek emperor was the creation of a buffer state between themselves and the barbarians to the north and east. With the example before them of the fate of Roman culture at the hands of the Goths and Vandals, they would not be likely to welcome the growing power of either the Scandinavians or the Pechenegs. By encouraging the pro-Slavonic and anti-Scandinavian elements in Kiev, they were supporting the growth of local interests and local patriotism, exactly as the Russians themselves are shown in the Kirghiz epic poems[1] to make use of native heroic elements among the Kirghiz in central Asia as a bulwark against the Chinese in the seventeenth century.

The picture of Vladimir I given in the *Povêst* certainly does not suggest a figure who would be likely to attract a heroic *comitatus*, or to be the focus of a Cycle of heroic poems. Neither Novgorod nor Kiev was won by his own efforts. Judged by any standards, his acquisition of the latter, according to the records, is a highly discreditable story. Except the subjugation of the scattered forest-dwelling population immediately to the west and north, he can claim few military successes won in fair fight. According to the *Povêst*, Oleg, Igor and Svyatoslav entered into political relations with the Greeks, and made treaties as a result of military activities; but Vladimir's relations with foreign

[1] I have discussed the policy of Russia in regard to the Kirghiz more fully in *The Growth of Literature*, Vol. III (Cambridge, 1940), p. 31.

powers, and especially with Byzantium, are represented in the *Povêst* as directed mainly to one end, and that end is not heroic but religious. It is with the aim of emphasising Vladimir's religious importance for Russia that the chronicler represents him as inordinately addicted to women in early life, as treacherous, idolatrous, and cruel. All is to point a contrast and add a lustre to his final conversion and sanctification. We see him, first as a sinner, later as a saint, but rarely as a hero, or as a man likely to have attracted heroes round him.

We must, however, beware of allowing ourselves to be influenced unduly by the evident 'purpose' which the chronicler has kept in view in writing the account of Vladimir's reign, and by the bias which this purpose has undoubtedly given to the facts. Unfortunately we have little independent evidence with which to compare and check the facts as he presents them. It is important, therefore, to make sure that we do not miss the true significance of these facts under the ecclesiastical colour in which they are invested. For instance one important incident, the true significance of which may easily escape us, is the account of Vladimir's communications with various neighbouring peoples, to which reference has already been made, and the various missions of these peoples to his court. These foreign missions are, characteristically enough, represented by the chronicler as purely religious in purpose. But we must not close our eyes to the fact that, whether we accept the traditions as having any solid foundation in fact or as merely the literary clichés and commonplaces of contemporary hagiology, they at any rate suggest by their very application to Vladimir that lively communications were established between Kiev and the neighbouring states in Vladimir's reign, and they might be represented in a secular, and more especially a heroic tradition, as indicating that Vladimir attracted foreigners to his court, such as, for example, the hero Khazarín, 'the Khazar', who figures in the *byliny*, side by side with Dyuk Stefanovich from Galicia and other strangers.

CHAPTER V

THE TREATIES WITH THE GREEKS,
AND RUSSIAN HEATHENISM

For the compiler of the *Povêst* the principal event of the reign of Vladimir I is his conversion to Christianity and the official inclusion of the Russian state in the Greek Orthodox Church. In order to throw this great historical event into better perspective, great emphasis is laid on Vladimir's earlier heathenism. A few brief but unequivocal notices of his discreditable relations with women in early life are entered by the chronicler manifestly in order to bring out, by force of contrast, the importance of his later piety. But the chronicler especially deploys the material at his disposal, which gives us a full and telling picture of Vladimir's heathen idols, and of their destruction immediately after the conversion. It is probable that a part of this story had already been incorporated into some form of 'Life of Saint Vladimir' before the *Povêst* took shape, and that it had, even in its earlier form, assumed something of the lurid colouring which it sheds over the pages of the chronicle. But there can be no possible doubt that the chronicler himself or his predecessor, the author of the 'Life', has derived his materials for this story wholly from traditional oral saga, and that, whatever its origin, the narrative owes many of its most striking features to the oral milieu through which it has been transmitted.

The story of Vladimir's idols is curious and interesting. There are three main references to Vladimir's idolatry. The first, which may be said to be the *locus classicus* for early Slavonic heathenism, is perhaps even more interesting for what it tells us of the heathen sanctuary than of the gods themselves. Here (s.a. 6486–6488, i.e. A.D. 978–980) we are told that after the murder of Yaropolk, 'Vladimir began to rule alone in Kiev, and he set up idols (*kumiri*) on the mound (*kholm*) outside the building (*dvor*) with the *terem*:[1] one of Perun, made of wood, with a head of silver and a moustache of gold, and others of Khors, Dazhbog, Stribog, Simargl and Mokosh. They sacrificed to them, calling them gods, and brought their sons and daughters to sacrifice them to demons. They polluted the earth with their sacrifice, and the Russian land and this hill were defiled with blood....Vladimir had appointed his uncle Dobrynya to rule over Novgorod. When Dobrynya came to Novgorod, he set up an idol (*kumir*) beside the river Volkhov, and the people of Novgorod sacrificed to it as if it were God'.[2]

Later, after Vladimir's baptism, we are told (s.a. 6496, A.D. 988) that when he arrived at his capital he gave orders that the *kumiri* (idols) should be overthrown, and that 'some should be cut to pieces and others burned with fire'. He thus ordered that Perun should be bound to a horse's tail and dragged down Borichev hill to the stream. 'He appointed twelve men to beat him with cudgels, and this, not on the supposition that the wood was sentient, but as an insult to the demon who had deceived men in this form, that he might receive requital from men.... While he was being dragged along the stream to the Dnêpr, unbelieving people lamented for him, for they had not yet received holy baptism. And having dragged him along they cast him into the Dnêpr.'[3]

From this passage it would seem probable that some of the idols were of stone and others of wood, Perun being of wood.

The passage is generally regarded as referring to the beating of the idol;[4] and it would be difficult, perhaps impossible, to interpret the reference to *yako drêvu chuyushchyu* as having application to anything other than the idol itself. Moreover, the fact that, in the Norse saga of Olaf Tryggvason contained in the

[1] '*I postavi kumiry na kholmu vnê dvora teremnago.*' It should be noted that the word used here and in most of the other passages cited below is *kholm*, 'mound', 'hillock', not *gora*, 'hill', 'mountain'.

[2] Miklosich, *Cronica Nestoris*, p. 46; Cross, *op. cit.* p. 180.

[3] Miklosich, *op. cit.* p. 71.

[4] For an interesting study on the subject which differs in its conclusions from my own, see A. H. Krappe, 'La Chute du Paganisme à Kiev', *Revue des Études Slaves*, Vol. XVII (1937), pp. 206 ff.

Flateyjarbók, Thorgerthr Hölgabrúthr, who is sometimes represented as an idol, is said to have been bound to a horse's tail by the Christian king, lends strong support to such an interpretation. It may indeed be doubted if the two traditions are wholly independent, since King Olaf is said to have spent his youth at Vladimir's court. It would, perhaps, be giving too much weight to the details of the tradition preserved in the *Povêst* to ask whether Olaf can have been present at Vladimir's missionary activities, and, on his return to Norway, have treated the heathen idol in the manner in which he had seen Perun treated in Russia.[1] It will readily be conceded, however, that this form of insult is not likely to have been a native one in Norway, which is not a country where customs connected with horses are likely to be indigenous, whereas we know that on the steppes and plains of Asia and eastern and central Europe this form of insult was particularly common, especially as inflicted on women. Thus a similar death is said to have been inflicted on the Frankish queen Brunhild at the hands of King Hlothair.[2] The Thuringians are credited by their Frankish enemies with having tied maidens by the arms to the necks of their horses, which were then driven in different directions.[3] Similarly, in the Yugoslav heroic poems, the hero Marko Kraljevich is said to punish the treachery of a girl by tying her to a horse's tail, and then driving it over the hills.[4]

Yet there are undoubtedly features in the Russian story which suggest that the victim of the Christian zeal of Vladimir is not

---

[1] According to the chronology of the *Povêst* and of the *Saga of King Olaf Tryggvason* contained in the *Heimskringla* this would not be impossible. No reliance can be placed on either chronology, however, or, from a historical point of view, on the actual treatment of the idols in either case. It may be added that according to the *Saga of Olaf Tryggvason* (*Heimskringla*), ch. 5, Olaf's maternal uncle had long been with King Vladimir in Russia.

[2] For references, see Gibbon, *Decline and Fall*, Vol. I, ch. 38.

[3] See Gregory of Tours, Vol. III, ch. 7.

[4] See *Hrvatske Narodne Pjesme* (published by the *Matica Hrvatska*), I, ii, 126 ff. For a brief summary of the story and references to variants, see Chadwick, *Growth of Literature*, Vol. II, p. 311.

the idol, but the priest of Perun. The idol would seem to be more naturally included in the toll of those 'cut to pieces and burnt'. The custom of dragging at a horse's tail is generally, as we have seen, a human punishment, despite the case of Thorgerthr Hölgabrúthr—if indeed this story does not also refer to a human being. The beating by twelve people specially assigned for the purpose suggests rather a priest whipped by his own immediate followers or by the temple staff. We may point to the 'council of twelve', which seems to have been an early and widespread feature of the Teutonic priesthood,[1] and to the twelve 'sons' traditionally ascribed by the chronicler Simon Grunau, a monk of Tolkemit, to Widowuto, the mythical king of the Old Prussians.[2]

In this connection attention may be called to an interesting passage in this same account of the Old Prussians by Grunau. He has left it on record that in 1520 he witnessed a sacrifice in the Old Prussian province of Samland, where a number of people were performing a sacrifice in honour of Percuno. The *waideler*, or 'priest' who presided, absolved the people from their sins, and immediately afterwards they all fell upon him, beating him and pulling his hair. We are told that the louder he shrieked, the more efficacious was their absolution. The ceremony also included the sacrifice of a goat.[3] It is clear that the *waideler* is here the chief participant in a scapegoat rite, and the story of the treatment of Perun has all the appearance of a genuine heathen tradition of a closely similar character, transformed by the Christian chronicler, as befits its place in his scheme of Vladimir's Christian activities. It may be added that if the ill-treatment is interpreted

---

[1] Chadwick, 'The Ancient Teutonic Priesthood', *Folklore*, Vol. XI (1900), p. 282. The number is not accidental. We may point to the consistency with which the numbers nine (or three) and seven occur in relation to the followers of the Asiatic shamans. Cf. further my article 'Shamanism among the Tatars of Central Asia', *Journal of the Royal Anthropological Institute*, Vol. LXVI (1936), pp. 87 ff.

[2] See Grunau, *Preussische Chronik*, Vol. I (Leipzig, 1876), Tractat II, ch. 4, pp. 68 ff.

[3] Grunau, *op. cit.*, Tractat III, pp. 90 f.

as applied to the idol and not to the priest, the final hurling of a wooden statue into the Dnêpr would be a futile way of endeavouring to compass its destruction. The story may have arisen to account for the local name 'Perun's Shore', where the idol is stated to have come to the bank after floating downstream for some time; but the death would in any case be more appropriate to Perun's priest than to Perun's idol, especially as the close connection of the god with the river is attested by the ancient position of his sanctuary on the hill above the river, as well as that ascribed to the idol said to have been set up by Dobrynya, Vladimir's uncle and *voevoda*, on the banks of the Volkhov at Novgorod.

Now apart from an obscure allusion to the 'idol of Tmutorakan' in the work known as the *Slovo o Polky Igorevê*, references to idols are extremely rare in early Russian literature, though we know from the narrative of the Arabic geographer Ibn Faḍlān[1] that the 'Rus' on the Volga possessed something in the nature of idols made of wood. References to human sacrifices are also practically unknown in early Russia. It is true that where so little has been preserved, little importance can be attached to negative

---

[1] Ahmed Ibn Faḍlān was sent in 921 by the Caliph Muqtadir as envoy to the Bulgars on the Volga, and on returning to Baghdad in 922 wrote an account of what he saw, part of which has survived in Yaqut's *Geographical Dictionary*, which dates from the early thirteenth century. The chief edition and complete translation (into German) easily accessible at the present time in the West is still C. M. Frähn, *Ibn Foszlans und anderer Araber Berichte über die Russen älterer Zeit* (St Petersburg, 1823). The reference to the 'Russian' wooden pillars bearing a rough semblance of a human face, and apparently reverenced by the 'Rus' on the Volga, will be found on pp. 7f. A recent edition has been published in Russia by Krachkovsky, which contains some additional paragraphs and an edition with German translation and commentary by A. Zeki Validi Togan in Leipzig in 1939. A large part of Ibn Faḍlān's narrative was published in an English translation (from a Danish translation) by Joseph Anderson in *Proceedings of the Society of Antiquaries of Scotland*, Vol. IX (1873), pp. 518ff. A recent translation, also of a large part of Ibn Faḍlān's narrative, from the original Arabic, is published by Charis Waddy under the title 'A Scandinavian Cremation Ceremony' in *Antiquity*, March 1934, pp. 58ff. Neither of the English translations contains the part of the narrative which speaks of the idols.

evidence, and Ibn Faḍlān's long and circumstantial account of the slaying of a girl in the same account of the 'Rus' on the Volga cannot be regarded as a religious sacrifice, though it is definitely ascribed to the 'Rus'. Whatever is exactly meant by the term 'Rus' here it can hardly be Slavonic, and it is generally considered to be Swedish.

The most curious feature of the idols of Vladimir is that they are represented, not as enclosed in a building, but as 'on a mound outside the *dvor* with the *terem*'. This *dvor* is a very interesting building, and we have had references to it before. It is earlier in this same entry that we are told that when Blud, Vladimir's *voevoda* in Kiev, lured Yaropolk into Vladimir's presence in order to destroy him, Vladimir, on hearing of his approach, 'went to his father's *dvor* with the *terem*, of which we previously made mention', and as Yaropolk entered the door, two Varangians[1] stabbed him under the arms with their swords, while Blud shut the doors to prevent his followers from entering. As suggested above (p. 37), if the place itself were appropriate, the details and the scene would almost suggest a ritual sacrifice rather than a murder. But what exactly is the '*dvor* with the *terem*' which has been 'previously mentioned'?

The most specific reference to this building occurs early in the *Povêst* in the story of Olga's vengeance against the Drevlians for the murder of her husband Igor (Norse Ingvarr), where circumstantial details of the royal city and dwellings are given. The scene has already been described (pp. 28 f. above);[2] and it has been pointed out that the burial of the ship's crew as they sit alive on the benches at their oars in the trench which had been dug in the *dvor* with the stone *terem* recalls the accounts of ship burials in stone barrows in the Norse sagas. The Russian description itself implies the scarcity of stone buildings, and we know that the royal residence itself was inside, not outside the city. The building with the stone hall must have been near the river bank, and the

---

[1] We may note the care with which the actual murder is laid at the door of the Norsemen, and not of the Slavs.

[2] Miklosich, *op. cit.* p. 31; Cross, *op. cit.* p. 165.

actual scene before us, as well as the later references, suggest that it may have been a great sanctuary.[1]

The building which we are discussing was in any case not new in Vladimir's day, for, as we have just seen, it is said to have been used as a place of sacrifice by Olga previously. Moreover, at the opening of the treaty which her husband Igor concluded with the Greeks in 945, and of which the text is transcribed in the *Povêst*, we find the words: 'If any inhabitant of the land of Rus thinks to violate this amity, may such of these transgressors as... be not baptised...receive help neither from God nor from Perun; may they not be protected by their own shields, but may they be slain by their own swords, laid low by their own arrows, or by any of their own weapons, and may they be in bondage for ever.'

And at the conclusion of the agreement: 'If any of the princes or any Russian subject, whether Christian or heathen, violates the terms of this agreement, he shall merit death by his own weapons, and be accursed of God and of Perun because he violated his oath.'[2]

Moreover, at the conclusion of the treaty we are told that, after summoning the Greek envoys, Igor 'went to the mound (or "hillock", *kholm*) where Perun stood. The Russes laid down their weapons, their shields, and their gold, and Igor and his people took the oath.'

That this is the same mound as that on which Vladimir's idols stood, there can be no doubt.[3] Apart from the reference to

---

[1] Can it possibly be the 'holy stone...among the Gothic peoples' referred to by Angantýr in the poem on the 'Battle of the Goths and Huns', contained in the *Hervarar Saga*? See Kershaw, *Anglo-Saxon and Norse Poems* (Cambridge, 1922), pp. 150 f., 202. Stone buildings were also rare in south Russia in early times. Sarkel, the famous stone fortress at the bend of the Don, was built by Greek engineers for the Khazars. Possibly the *dvor* with the stone *terem* at Kiev was of similar origin.

[2] Miklosich, *op. cit.* p. 26; Cross, *op. cit.* p. 160.

[3] It will be noticed that the same word (*kholm*, 'mound', 'hillock') is used, though in the passage describing Olga's vengeance against the Drevlians in their ship the word used is *gora*, 'hill'; but the place is avowedly the same.

Perun, we are also told that the Christians, i.e. the Greek envoys (and possibly some local Varangian Christians), 'took oath in the Church of St Elias, which is above the stream in the vicinity of the place of the Pasynchi (Pechenegs?) and of the Khazars'.[1] It may be safely assumed that the 'place of the Pechenegs and the Khazars' would be by the ford referred to in the story of Olga at the foot of the mound on which stood the *dvor* with the stone *terem*, outside which the statues of Perun and of the other gods are said to have stood later in the time of Vladimir I.

The treaty which, according to the text of the *Povêst*, Oleg made with the Greeks at an earlier date (904–907) had been confirmed by a similar oath; but here the name Volos has been added to that of Perun. The chronicler tells us that Oleg and his retinue, in confirmation of this treaty, 'according to the religion of the Rus, swore by their weapons and by their god Perun, as well as by Volos, the god of wealth (or 'herds', *skotinim bogom*),[2] and thus confirmed the treaty'.[3]

Similarly Svyatoslav, Igor's son, in concluding a treaty with the Greeks in 6479 (A.D. 971), after swearing to preserve the treaty inviolate, continues in these terms: 'If we fail...may we be accursed by the god in whom we believe, namely by Perun and Volos, the god of wealth (*skoti bog*), and may we be struck as gold is struck, and be cut to pieces by our own weapons.'[4]

From this it would seem that Perun and Volos are two deities

---

[1] Miklosich, *op. cit.* p. 30; Cross, *op. cit.* p. 164. The Pasynchi are not known. Can the word be a form of *Patzinak*, i.e. 'Pecheneg'?

[2] The words in the Russian text are in the dative case, the nominative being *skoti bog*, which is generally translated 'the god of flocks', or 'of herds'. The word *skot-* is a loan-word from Teutonic. Cf. Gothic *skatts*, Anglo-Saxon *sceatt*, both of which words generally have reference to money. For an analogous development we may compare the history of the Anglo-Saxon word *feoh* (Latin *pecus*), which originally meant 'flock', later, 'property', 'money'; cf. also pp. 88 f. below.

[3] Miklosich, *op. cit.* p. 16; Cross, *op. cit.* p. 151.

[4] Miklosich, *op. cit.* p. 42; Cross, *op. cit.* p. 176. I have followed the reading of the Laurentian text, which has *budem koloti*, 'may we be struck' (as gold is struck).

habitually coupled together in early Varangian oaths, which are also sworn on weapons, the latter apparently forming the third element in such oaths. Even if we suppose the account of Oleg's treaty and oath to be secondary, and composed by the chronicler on the model of the later treaties and oath,[1] the evidence of the traditional formula and of Svyatoslav's oath is in no way impaired.

Now there can be little doubt that these Varangian oaths contain references to the three principal Norse gods Thor, Freyr and Óthinn, in this order. They evidently follow a fixed formula, and seem to correspond exactly to the official form of oath taken by the people of Iceland in heathen times. In the *Hauksbók* text of the *Landnámabók*, ch. 268, we are told that in the preamble to the heathen laws it was stated that a ring weighing at least two ounces should be on the altar of every temple, and that oaths should be sworn on that ring, and in the presence of witnesses the juror should say: 'I swear an oath upon the ring—a lawful oath; so help me Freyr and Njörthr, and the almighty god (*hinn almáttki áss*).'

Despite the fact that the term 'almighty god' has sometimes been thought to refer to Óthinn, there can be no doubt whatever that Thor is the god indicated. The Icelandic settlers were drawn from the *hersar* and the *bœndr*, that is to say, from the landowners and small farmers, whose special god Thor was, and not from the military aristocracy, who favoured Óthinn. Can the ring used in the Icelandic oaths here and elsewhere[2] be a symbolic remnant of gold treasure such as that referred to in Igor's oath?

In the treaties of the Norse rulers of Kiev with the Greeks, the name of Perun has been substituted for that of Thor by an easy transition. In Scandinavian lands Thor is the thunder god. The name of the Russian Perun is surely to be equated with the name

---

[1] See especially Mansikka, *Die Religion der Ostslaven* (Helsinki, 1922), pp. 30, 33.

[2] We may compare, for example, the early Norse poem the *Hávamál*, str. 110, contained in the *Elder Edda*: 'I suppose that Óthinn had sworn a ring oath. How can his word be trusted?'

of the Lithuanian god Perkunas,[1] despite the philological difficulty of the loss of the -k-. Perkunas is the Lithuanian god of the
thunder, and according to Procopius, who wrote during the
sixth century, the Slavs (Sklavenoi) still worshipped 'one god, the
creator of the lightning', whom they 'believe to be the sole lord
of all, and they sacrifice to him oxen and all offerings'.[2]

In all probability this is Perun, and the Varangians of Kiev
have not been slow to translate the name of their own thunder
god into that of the corresponding deity in the country of their
adoption.

There can, I think, be little doubt that the oath taken on the
weapons in the ratification of the Scandinavian treaties with the
Greeks contains a tacit reference to Óthinn, the god of battle,
and the special deity of the Norse military class. The omission
of his name in the oaths is not surprising, for he is more often
referred to in early Norse literature by some epithet, or veiled
descriptive term, than under his own name. Indeed a kind of
tabu seems to have attached to it, like that on the name of Shaitan
among the Kurdish tribes known as Yezidi. Yet the act of laying
down their shields and weapons and swearing by them, and the
curse that in case of falsifying the covenant the conjurors shall
be 'slain by their own weapons' must surely have direct reference
to Óthinn.[3]

---

[1] He is closely associated with the oak. The name corresponds to Latin
quercus. For further details see Chadwick, 'The Oak and the Thunder
God', in the J.R.A.I. (1900), pp. 22 ff.

[2] Gothic War, III, 14.

[3] We may compare a passage from Ammianus Marcellinus (XVII,
xii, 21) with reference to the Quadi, a Suevic (Teutonic) people living
near the source of the Elbe, but very much associated with the Sarmatians
who were Iranians. Here we are told that the Quadi 'promised obedience;
and gave their children as hostages for the performance of the conditions
imposed upon them; and drawing their swords, which they worship as
deities, they swore to remain faithful'. The information is, however,
possibly derived by Ammianus from the account of the Scythians given by
Herodotus, IV, 62. We may compare also what is said by the same writer
(XXXI, ii, 23) of the Sarmatians themselves: 'Nor is there any temple
or shrine seen in their country, nor even any cabin thatched with straw,

Who then is Volos, whose attributes appear to have required specification to the Russians of the early twelfth century, but who seems to have been perfectly familiar to Svyatoslav, and who also appears in the treaty attributed to Oleg? The name corresponds exactly to the name of a certain Norse fetich Völsi, and to the mythical founder of the early Norse legendary family known as the Völsungar, whose traditional date would fall in the fourth century. The cult of Völsi is referred to in a brief story contained in the longer version of the Saga of King Olaf Tryggvason preserved in the manuscript known as the *Flateyjarbók* already referred to above. In this story a fetich, consisting of the genital organs of a horse called Völsi, plays a leading role (cf. p. 155 below). Other allusions to the cult can be traced in the same saga.[1] A comparison of these references with the opening chapters of the *Völsungasaga* leaves little room to doubt that Völsi is only another and less usual name for the Norse god Freyr.[2] This would seem to justify us in enquiring whether Volos and Freyr have anything in common.

The word *Freyr* means simply 'lord', and the same god is also known by other names, which are sometimes compounded with Freyr, as, for example, Yngvi-Freyr. His cult seems to be practically identical with that of Nerthus, a goddess, mentioned in the

their only idea of religion being to plunge a naked sword into the ground with barbaric ceremonies, and then they worship that with great respect as Mars, the presiding deity of the regions over which they wander.' In connection with this last statement we may refer to a passage by Jordanes (cap. xxxv) in which he relates that a sword, attributed to the Scythians, was found protruding from the soil by one of Attila's shepherds. The importance which Attila attached to this sword, and to its possession as a happy omen, suggests that it was looked upon as something more than a mere chance find.

[1] I have worked out the evidence for associating certain allusions in this saga with the cult of Freyr more fully in my forthcoming book referred to above (p. 22).

[2] The generative aspect of Freyr is emphasised by Adam of Bremen, IV, 26 f. For an interesting note on the phallic aspect of the god, see Turville-Petre, 'The Cult of Freyr in the Evening of Paganism', in *Proceedings of the Leeds Philosophical and Literary Society*, 1935, p. 321.

Germania of Tacitus, whose chief sanctuary is said to have been on an island, perhaps the island of Sjaelland.[1] On the other hand Freyr seems also to be identical with the early mythical Danish peace king, Frith-Fróthi, of whom Saxo Grammaticus has left us an account. In the form Yngvi-Freyr, or Ingunar-Freyr, he is probably to be connected with Ing, who in the Old English Runic poem is located among the 'East Danes', who again are almost certainly included among the Ingvaeones of Tacitus. These in their turn seem to comprise Danes and other maritime peoples. The chief seat of the cult of Freyr is said to have been at Uppsala in Sweden, however,[2] and there is reason to believe that it reached Sweden from the south, perhaps from north Germany, perhaps partly through Gautland in the south of Sweden, where the cult seems to have been deeply rooted.[3] From Sweden it spread to Norway and Iceland. It is especially associated with the cult of horses,[4] but oxen were sacrificed to him.[5]

It is stated by Snorri Sturluson, a Norse antiquarian writer of the first half of the thirteenth century, in his account of the early kings of Sweden, that Freyr was a 'temple priest' who ruled in Sweden. 'He was called the "lord of the Swedes", and took free tribute (*skattr*) from them.' And when he fell ill, they built a big barrow for him with a door and three windows, and after his death they carried him into the barrow secretly, and hid his death

[1] See H. M. Chadwick, *The Origin of the English Nation* (Cambridge, 1907), pp. 207 ff. Cf. also B. Dickins, *Runic and Heroic Poems* (Cambridge, 1915), p. 20, note 67.

[2] See H. M. Chadwick, 'The Ancient Teutonic Priesthood', *Folk Lore*, Vol. XI (1900), pp. 292 ff.

[3] See Turville-Petre, *loc. cit.* pp. 328 f.

[4] We may refer to the stud of horses sacred to Freyr, kept at Trondhjem (*Flat.* I, p. 403), and also to that of Hrafnkels Freysgothi in Iceland (see *Hrafnkels Saga Freysgotha*). We may refer further to the horse known as Freyfaxi, and evidently sacred to Freyr, also in Iceland, mentioned in *Vatnsdaela Saga*, ch. xxxiv, 6.

[5] See *Víga Glums Saga*, ch. 9. In connection with the oxen sacrificed to Freyr, and the horses which are said to be sacred to him, we may compare what is said below about Volos.

from the Swedes for three years,[1] 'and poured all the tribute (*skattr*) into the mound, gold through one window, silver through another, and copper pennies through a third'. And in the meantime peace and plenty reigned.[2]

Turning now once more to the gods of ancient Kiev, we are told that in the oath taken by Igor on the mound on which Perun stood, the 'Rus' laid down, not only their shields and weapons, but also their gold, and that then they took their oath. If I am right in regarding the weapons as symbolical of Óthinn, and in equating Perun and Volos with Thor and Freyr, is it not possible that the gold has direct relation to Freyr? Thus each god referred to in the oath is represented by a symbol—Thor by the statue of Perun, with silver head[3] and golden whiskers; Othinn by shields and weapons; and Freyr by gold—all of which symbols are apparently referred to in the oaths, either specifically, or by indirect reference. From this it is clear that the curse in Svyatoslav's treaty to the effect that, in the event of their breaking their pledged word, they shall become yellow as gold, and fall by their own weapons, contains a direct reference, not only to Óthinn, but to Volos (Freyr) also.[4] It will be remembered that Volos, whom I have identified with Freyr, is twice referred to as *skoti bog*. The word is glossed 'cattle', 'flocks' in the dictionary, and such is no doubt its modern meaning;[5] but it seems to be a

---

[1] It is perhaps worth noting that in the *Povêst*, s.a. 6523 (A.D. 1015), the death and burial of Vladimir I is similarly kept a secret by his followers, though we are not told for how long. The context suggests that it was for some considerable period of time. The death of Prince Mstislav, the son of Svyatopolk, is also said (s.a. 6605, i.e. A.D. 1097) to have been concealed from his people by his followers, but in this case the concealment is only for three days.

[2] *Ynglinga Saga* (*Heimskringla*), ch. 12.

[3] We may compare the statue to Jómali in the Icelandic Saga of Herrauðr and Bósi.

[4] I see no ground for the suggestion that the reference to gold is a specifically Russian formula, as suggested by Mansikka (*op. cit.* p. 37). The views of Rozniecki and Tiander are equally improbable (see Mansikka, *loc. cit.* footnote 2).

[5] The word *skotnitsa* seems to mean 'treasury', as well as 'neatherd'.

loan word from a Teutonic word which appears in O.E. *sceatt*,[1] Gothic *skatts*, 'dinarion'. This O.E. word is the name of a certain coin in Anglo-Saxon times, and it is also used in the more general sense of tribute. The word is also common in early Norse in the form *skattr*, used most commonly in the sense of 'tribute'. We have just seen it used in this sense in the passages quoted above with reference to Freyr. Is it not possible, therefore, that the Russian epithet of Volos (*skoti bog*) is used in this same sense in our text?

It is noteworthy that the name of Volos is omitted from Vladimir's list of idols. This can hardly be due to inadvertence, in view of the important position which he holds in the oaths, and it requires explanation. Now the name which immediately follows Perun in the list is Khors. This name, which is not unknown elsewhere,[2] has never been identified. The form, however, is an exact equivalent of the A.S. *hors*, O.N. *hross*, 'a horse', and in view of the Völsi fetish, and a whole mass of other Scandinavian evidence which might be adduced connecting the cult of Freyr with the horse,[3] I suggest that it is a possible reference to Volos or Freyr, hence its position next to Perun.

The testimony of the oaths is more in conformity with archaeological discovery than is the pantheon of Vladimir's idols at the sanctuary of Kiev. It is said[4] that in hardly any case has more

[1] We may compare the variation in meaning in Anglo-Saxon *feoh*, which had the sense of both 'cattle' and 'money'. Cf. p. 83 above.

[2] E.g. in the *Slovo o Polku Igorevê*, l. 596, and elsewhere; see Magnus, note *ad loc.*

[3] As one instance only I may refer to the Icelandic *Hrafnkels Saga Freysgotha*, in which we are told that Hrafnkell kept a stud of horses, one stallion of which, called Freyfaxi ('Freyr mane'), was sacred to Freyr, and must never be mounted. Cf. also p. 62 above. The Russian name *Khors* is frequently identified with the Persian word خورشید (*khorshid*, 'the Sun'), and treated as evidence of sun worship among the ancient Slavs. I see no justification for this identification, which seems to me extremely improbable both in itself and also on philological grounds.

[4] See Cross, *op. cit.* p. 119, footnote, and the references there cited. See especially A. Brückner, 'Mythologische Thesen', *Archiv für slavische Philologie*, Vol. XL (1926), p. 9.

than one idol been discovered in any one sanctuary excavated. Is it possible that, apart from Perun, the other gods were represented, not by anthropomorphic statues, but by fetiches or symbols, like Völsi? The reference to Volos under the term 'Horse' would thus be more easily understandable, and exactly parallel to the incident of the Norse Völsi mentioned above. It is, indeed, possible that Volos was not familiar to the early Russians under his own name. In both the oaths in which he is referred to specifically by name, the chronicler has added the words *skoti bog*, as if the name required further definition in order to be readily identifiable by the reader[1]—and this, despite the large part which he has come to play in modern folk-lore, perhaps, as has been suggested, by confusion with St Blaise.[2]

The most peculiar feature about Vladimir's sanctuary is that the idols are said to be, not inside, but outside the '*dvor* with the stone *terem*'. This feature is in striking contrast to Scandinavian accounts of idols which the Norsemen are represented in the sagas as finding in the temples of Bjarmaland, and in their eastward journeys generally. Yet it is not an isolated notice, for, as we have seen, Dobrynya is said to have set up an idol[3] on the bank of the river Volkhov at Novgorod—apparently a very similar site. We may, however, compare the religious practices of the Lithuanians and the Old Prussians, who, we are told, had no temples but worshipped in sacred groves, and among whom also we find references to sacred hills and lakes.[4]

Still the most remarkable feature of Vladimir's sanctuary

[1] It is, of course, possible that the term *skoti bog* is a static epithet of Volos, and invariably attached to his name; but this would be unusual in the case of a god.

[2] The names are obviously identical, as Mansikka (*op. cit.* pp. 34, 40) points out, and as is generally agreed. But that the name of the deity mentioned in the oaths has been derived from the Christian saint is, from every point of view, extremely improbable.

[3] According to the Hypatian text of the *Povêst*, this was also an idol to Perun. The Laurentian text omits the name of the god.

[4] See the articles by Bezzenberger on 'Lithuanians' and by Welsford on 'Old Prussians' and 'Serpent Worship' in Hastings' *Encyclopedia of Religion and Ethics*, and the references there cited.

remains the number of idols which it is said to have contained. These, as we have seen, are six in number, namely Perun, Khors, Dazhbog, Stribog, Simargl and Mokosh. The number is the more surprising in view of the fact that, as we have already observed, archaeological evidence suggests that in general only one statue was contained in any given sanctuary.[1] Even if the identifications which I have suggested above were accepted, and even if it were conceded, as I have also suggested, that in Vladimir's sanctuary also Perun alone was represented by an idol, and the remaining gods only by fetiches or symbols, the number would still require explanation. The great Swedish temple at Uppsala is stated by Adam of Bremen to have had three idols— to Thor, Óthinn and Freyr. The great Lithuanian forest sanctuary at Romové also contained the representations of three human heads carved in the trunk of the sacred oak, which are said to have represented the gods Perkunas, Patollo and Potrimpo.

Now according to Lucas David,[2] a very reliable authority of the sixteenth century, the most important of these deities was Patollo, though it is always Perkunas who is said to communicate with the chief priest by means of thunder and lightning. Of the identification of Perkunas with the Russian Perun and the Norse Thor we have already spoken, and there can, I think, be no serious doubt on this point, despite the philological difficulty. In addition, Patollo—'Patollos or Pickollos'[3]—may with equal certainty be identified with Óthinn. He is described as 'the chief god of the Old Prussians', and he was regarded as 'the god of death', and as 'having power to kill'. His name, under the form 'Pecols

---

[1] Cf. also pp. 89 f. above.

[2] *Preussische Chronik*, ed. Hennig (Königsberg, 1812), Vol. I, p. 33.

[3] Casp. Schütz, *Hist. Rer. Pruss.* 1599, p. 26 (see *Archiv f. slav. Philol.* XVIII, p. 80). There is obvious confusion in the forms; but this need not be regarded very seriously, since all Lithuanian proper names recorded in early times show an exceptional amount of variation in the transcription, probably due to the fact that the language was not standardised or even recorded in writing until a late date. It should, however, be noted that in the opinion of Miss Welsford at least two distinct deities are included under these names.

atque Pocols', is glossed as *Pluto, Furiae*,[1] and again: 'Pocclum inferni ac tenebrarum deum', and 'Pocollom aereorum spirituum deum';[2] and finally 'Pocullus deus inferorum et tenebrarum... Pocullus deus spirituum volantium sive cacodaemonarum'.[3] According to Praetorius,[4] the heads of a horse and a cow were an acceptable offering to Pikullis[5] (i.e. Patollo), and we are told that at Romové, the chief sanctuary of the Old Prussians, the heads of a horse, a cow and a man were placed before Patollo as his particular treasure.[6] Patollo and Potrimpo are said to have had a special taste for human blood.[7] This close connection with the dead and the inimical powers of the Underworld points strongly to an identification with the Norse god Óthinn, the god of the dead and the direct agent of slaughter and of bloodshed.

These references to Patollo do not exhaust the evidence for his connection with the land of the dead. Elsewhere Grunau speaks of a 'banner' (*bannir*) of white cloth on which were pictured three portrait busts. Two of these, we are told, were Potrimpo and Patollo, while the description of the third makes it clear that he is Perkunas. Patollo was represented as an old man with a long beard. His colour was deathly, and he was crowned with a white cloth like a 'morbant'.[8] It is interesting to note that

[1] Constit. Synod. Evangel. 1530 (see *Archiv f. slav. Philol.* xvIII, p. 77, footnote 1).

[2] Meletius; see *Archiv f. slav. Philol.* xvIII, p. 76.

[3] Waissel, *Chron. Pruss.* 1599 (see *Archiv f. slav. Philol.* xvIII, p. 79). Cf. Norse Óthinn, *Wodan, id est 'furor'* (Adam of Bremen, IV, 20). See H. M. Chadwick, *The Cult of Othinn* (Cambridge, 1899), p. 67.

[4] *Deliciae Prussicae* (ed. Pierson, Berlin, 1871).

[5] The word appears to be connected with Lithuanian *Pekla*, Latvian *Pekle*, Russian *Peklo*, 'Hell'.

[6] Grunau, *Preussische Chronik* (Leipzig, 1876), I, 5, § 2.

[7] Lucas David, *Preussische Chronik*, Vol. I, p. 34.

[8] *Preussische Chronik*, I, 5, § 1. With the account of the *bannir* described by Grunau it is interesting to compare the account contained in the *Povést* (s.a. 6494, i.e. A.D. 986) of the *zapon* ('hanging', or 'wrapping', here perhaps a tapestry curtain) on which was pictured (*napisano*) the Day of Judgment. This *zapon* is stated to have been shown by a Greek scholar to Vladimir I in the course of his conversion. The scholar showed him on the right the blessed going to bliss in Paradise, and on the left the sinners going to torment. There can be no doubt that embroideries, owing to their

he is pictured as below the other two in the space on the 'banner', and as looking up at them. This fact may possibly be taken to indicate that he is underground, and so to emphasise his connection with the dead—a connection which is certainly emphasised by Grunau in this description as a whole. The connection between Patollo and Óthinn may be regarded as established, just as that between Perkunas (Perkun) and Thor.

Now Grunau has left us also a very interesting description of both Perkunas, who is not here mentioned by name, and also of Potrimpo, as they are pictured on this same banner. On his account of the picture of Perkunas I shall not dwell, since his close connection with Thor is generally accepted; but the account of Potrimpo is of great importance, since it is probably the fullest which we possess of this god, and is relevant to our study. The head, so Grunau tells us, was that of a young man without beard, crowned with ears of corn, and wearing a joyous expression. He was the god of corn, and he was pictured as laughing at his companion, who is represented as wearing an angry expression, and who, from the general description, is obviously Perkunas. With the association of Potrimpo with corn, which Grunau emphasises here, we may compare the descriptions of the sanctuary of Romové or Rickoyot given by Grunau (I, p. 78) and David (I, pp. 28 ff.), where we are told that the treasure placed before the image of Potrimpo was a snake which was kept in a jar or cruse (*toppe*) crowned with a bundle of corn.

There can, I think, be little doubt that Potrimpo is to be connected with the god Freyr. Freyr, as we have seen, is represented as a youthful and pleasure-loving god, the god of fertility both in human beings and in nature. The Swedes used to sacrifice to him for good seasons and crops (*til árs*), while in more than

---

durability and portability, have played a large part in the missionary enterprise of the early church, and that they would not be without their effect on heathen cultures also. The important part played by sewing in the development and spread of early Christian art shows itself plainly in the designs, appliqué and stitches being widely reflected in the paintings of the period, such as e.g. those in the Book of Kells and the Book of Deer.

one passage we are told that the snow would never lie on his barrow. He is essentially a god of rebirth. And I have no doubt that stories of snake cults, such as we find in the family history of Ragnarr Lothbrók, of the Völsungar, and elsewhere in early Norse literature, are directly connected with the cult of Freyr, as I hope to demonstrate more fully elsewhere.[1] The similarities between Freyr and Potrimpo on the one hand, and Freyr and Volos on the other, are too close to be accidental.

Now we have seen that, according to the *Povêst*, Vladimir's sanctuary contained six deities, several of which are unidentified. We have also seen that three of these deities seem to correspond to the Norse gods Thor,[2] Óthinn and Freyr, and also to the Old Prussian deities Perkunas, Patollo and Potrimpo. Whether we suppose that Vladimir, according to the Saga embedded in the *Povêst*, adopted the Norse pantheon direct from the Varangians, or whether, through the Drevlian parentage ascribed to him in the *Povêst*, we suppose that his deities have been influenced by his neighbours the Yatvings (who are themselves Lithuanians), and that he borrowed the gods, not directly in their Norse, but in their Old Prussian form, the number six is still unexplained. Is it possible that the two trilogies have been amalgamated and that the triad of deities has been duplicated? Is it possible that not only the Norse deities have been ascribed to Vladimir by tradition, or by a chronicler eager to make the most of the saint's

[1] I.e. in the book now in preparation and already referred to.

[2] The priority of Thor or Perun, implied by the Russian tradition, is important, and makes it fairly clear that the Scandinavian religious influence in Russia, even in Kiev itself, was not southern Norwegian but rather from Sweden and perhaps also Hálogaland. Adam of Bremen tells us that in the great temple at Uppsala the image of Thor occupied the central position, the images of Óthinn and Fricco (Freyr) being placed on his right and left. In Hálogaland also Thor was the chief god worshipped. The chief god of the Norwegian aristocracy of the south was Óthinn. Incidentally it is stated in the Norse Saga of Ketill Hængr, the grandfather of Örvar-Oddr (see p. 25 above), that even the mention of Óthinn's name made Ketill very angry, which is not unnatural, as he was an independent ruler in Hálogaland in the north of Norway, and had relations chiefly with Sweden.

early heathen activities, but that also their Lithuanian counter-
parts have been added to these?

In view of the sparsity of our evidence, and of the almost total
obscurity attaching to the names of most of Vladimir's deities,
the point must remain quite uncertain. But it is in itself by no
means impossible in any case, in view of his own connections,
that Vladimir may have introduced some cult allied to that of
the Lithuanians and Old Prussians into Kiev. In this connection
I may refer to another entry in the *Povêst*, s.a. 6491 (A.D. 983),
where we read: 'Vladimir marched on the Yatvings, conquered
them, and seized their land and returned to Kiev, and together
with his followers made sacrifice to the idols (*kumiri*).'[1]

The juxtaposition of these two statements may be merely
accidental; but it is certainly arresting. The passage continues:
'The elders and the *boyars* then said: "Let us cast lots for a youth
and a maiden and let us sacrifice to the gods whomsoever the
lot should fall upon."'

Immediately afterwards we are told that the lot fell upon a
young Varangian boy, whose father refused to give him up to be
sacrificed, because he was a Christian.

These are not isolated notices in the *Povêst*. In an earlier entry,
immediately after the enumeration of Vladimir's idols (cf.
p. 77 above), we have seen that the chronicler declares that the
people sacrificed to them and brought their sons and daughters
'to sacrifice them to demons', adding that 'they polluted the
earth with their sacrifices, and the Russian land and this hill were
defiled with blood'.[2]

Now this custom of human sacrifice is not common in the early
annals of either Russia or Scandinavia.[3] But strangely enough

---

[1] Miklosich, *op. cit.* p. 48; cf. Cross, *op. cit.* p. 182.

[2] The passage is, of course, quoted from the Bible, Psalm cvi, vv. 37, 38;
but the chronicler has added the reference to Russia and the specific 'hill'
(*kholm*).

[3] The account of the death of the girl among the 'Rus' on the Volga
as related by Ibn Faḍlān (see p. 80 above) must not be forgotten. This,
however, is an instance of suttee, or voluntary immolation, rather than of

it recalls a passage in early Norse literature which refers to the same part of the world as that of the Drevlians. In *Hervarar Saga*, ch. 7, we are told that a great famine arose in Reithgotaland, and threatened to destroy all the inhabitants. So they tried divination, and the answer was that there would be no plenty in Reithgotaland till the noblest boy in the land had been sacrificed (*blótat*). The word Reithgotaland in this passage is explained in the text itself at this point as having reference to Jutland; but in ch. 9 of the same saga, and elsewhere, the people in question are referred to as Gotar, i.e. the Goths. The earliest occurrence of the word gives the form Hraithgotum (dat. pl.),[1] which suggests that the name may be connected with *Hrethgotan*, a name applied to the Goths in Anglo-Saxon poetry. The Goths, whose home was in Poland, had expanded southwards and south-east-wards in the third and fourth centuries and are said to have had most of south Russia under their sway. Nevertheless a great number must have remained behind in the basin of the Vistula, and these are the Goths to whom the passage in the *Hervarar Saga* has reference. The Goths of south Russia either fled before the Huns, who appeared from the East c. 370, or soon became subject to them. On the other hand we know that a large and very flourishing community of Goths had settled in the west of the Crimea, in the district known as the *Klima*,[2] and that they continued to preserve their nationality and their identity even down to the seventeenth century. These Crimean Goths must have plied up and down the Dnêpr as traders throughout the Viking Age and later, and indeed there is interesting evidence suggesting that Hellenised Goths from the Crimea were not unknown as traders in Novgorod in the early part of the twelfth century.[3]

human sacrifice. Mansikka regards the whole account of human sacrifice under Vladimir in the *Povêst* as of literary origin, derived ultimately from Greek sources. See *Die Religion der Ostslaven*, pp. 40f.

[1] In the Swedish Runic inscription of Rök; cf. also the early Norse poem *Vafthrúthnismál*, str. 12.

[2] See A. A. Vasiliev, *The Goths in the Crimea* (Cambridge, Mass.), p. 96.

[3] See *ib.* p. 137. Vasiliev refers to a passage in the *Life of St Antonius the Roman*, where we are told that in 1106, when the saint came to

These various considerations make it not impossible that the human sacrifices ascribed by the chronicler to St Vladimir are based on traditions derived from traces of the religious practices of the scattered remnants of the earlier population to the west of Kiev. There is ample evidence for human sacrifices among the Old Prussians,[1] who were near neighbours of the Lithuanians and the Slavs to the west of Kiev, such as the Drevlians and Krivichians. Like the latter also they were forest peoples. If, therefore, it were in any way possible to accept the statement of the chronicler that human sacrifices were in fact a part of the religious practices of Kiev in the time of Vladimir I, we must regard it as, on the whole, most probable, either that the practices had been inherited from the more backward forest-dwelling Drevlians, or that they had been acquired from the practices of the Gothic or the Lithuanian peoples to the north-west, who had not come under the influence of Greek civilisation. My own belief is, however, that elements of both Khazar and Greek civilisation were too strong in tenth-century Kiev to make such a practice thinkable, and it is more natural to suppose that in this, as in much of the early part of the *Povêst*, the compiler is either incorporating motifs derived from oral tradition, and not necessarily of even local origin; or else—and this is perhaps more probable in view of the context—that he is drawing directly from Greek sources.[2]

Novgorod on a stone which floated upon the water, he met a merchant who spoke 'Roman, Greek and Russian', and who is described variously as *Gotfin*, *Grechanin* and *Grechanin-Gotfin*, which Vasiliev interprets as a Hellenised Crimean Goth. The *Life* has come down to us only in versions of the sixteenth to the eighteenth centuries, but is attributed to one Andrew, Antonius' disciple and successor as Abbot (Igumen) of the Monastery of the Holy Mother of God in Novgorod. See Vasiliev, *loc. cit.*

[1] The papal bull issued by Honorius III in 1218 contains a statement that the Old Prussians offered human sacrifices to their gods. Cf. further Lucas David, Vol. 1, p. 34; cf. p. 92 above.

[2] See Mansikka, as cited p. 95, footnote 3 above.

CHAPTER VI

YAROSLAV THE WISE

On the death of Vladimir a reaction set in, and the annals of the
Povêst amply support the statement of the Greek writer Psellos [1]
that the Russians were always hostile, and feverishly seeking
pretexts for hostilities. Vladimir was succeeded by his son
Svyatopolk, who allied himself with the Pechenegs, and also
with the Poles, who had recently been converted to the Roman
form of Christianity. He is hated by the chronicler no less for
these anti-Orthodox alliances than for the murder of his brothers,
the Orthodox Christians, Boris and Gleb, who were afterwards
canonised, and in the Annals of the *Povêst* he is statically referred
to as the 'accursed' (*okayanny*) Svyatopolk. Svyatopolk also
murdered his brother Svyatoslav, while a fourth brother Yaroslav, hearing that Svyatopolk was plotting against his life also,
collected an army composed of Varangians and soldiers of
Novgorod, and marched against Svyatopolk, whose army was
stationed on the eastern bank of the Dnêpr, and consisted of
Pechenegs and 'Rus'.

It would seem from the text that Yaroslav or his Varangian
mercenaries fought somewhat reluctantly, for on the day preceding the battle Svyatopolk's general is reported to have ridden
out along the shore and scoffed at the men of Novgorod,
shouting: 'Why did you come here with this lame fellow? [2] We
shall make you carpenters to fashion our houses.' Whereupon the
men of Novgorod are reported to have said to Yaroslav: 'To-
morrow we will cross over to them and whoever will not go
with us, we will kill'; and the next day, after crossing the Dnêpr,

---

[1] *Chronographie*, Vol. II, p. 8.

[2] The body of Yaroslav has been found, and it has been ascertained
that he was in fact lame. See *Kratkie Soobshcheniya o Dokladakh i Polevikh
Issledovanyakh Instituta Istorii Materialnoy Kultury*, Vol. VII (Moscow, 1940),
pp. 46 ff.

the men of Novgorod pushed the boats out from the bank after disembarking, in order to ensure that Yaroslav and his Varangians should not retreat. Their resolution was rewarded with complete victory. Svyatopolk fled to the Poles and Yaroslav reigned in Kiev, after having been in Novgorod twenty-eight years.

Two years later Svyatopolk returned to the attack with Boleslav of Poland as his ally. This time Yaroslav had his *voevoda* and *kormilets* ('fosterer', 'provisor') Budy with him, who is represented in the *Povêst* as having returned the previous insult which had been hurled at Yaroslav's physical defect by scoffing at the corpulent Boleslav with the words: 'We shall pierce your fat belly with a pike.' The insults and the form in which the whole narrative is couched are so close to the terse and biting wit of Norse skaldic poetry that it is difficult to believe the passage is not a literal translation from Norse. Boleslav was victorious, despite the taunt, and Yaroslav fled to Novgorod, planning to abandon all and depart to Sweden; but the *posadnik* or 'governor' Constantine, son of Dobrynya, together with the men of Novgorod, destroyed his boats and forced him to renew the fight. To this end they collected *skot* ('payment') 'at the rate of four skins per man, ten *grivni* from each elder, and eighteen *grivni* from each *boyar*'. With this *skot* they recruited an army of Varangians, whom they imported, and thus enlarged that of Yaroslav. It will be remembered that Vladimir's Varangian supporters in Kiev had previously claimed to be allowed a fixed proportion of payment from the citizens of Kiev. The clear testimony of the *Povêst* that both Vladimir and Yaroslav were almost wholly dependent on Scandinavian mercenaries, and that these were paid, not by foreign gold, but by the taxes levied on the local populace and local Slavonic aristocracy, is extremely interesting and important as helping to explain the position of the Scandinavian princes of the house of Rurik and their relationship to the existing order and social classes. Up to now the weakness of Yaroslav's position was that he was waging an uneven war with only the native troops of Novgorod (some 40,000 men) and about 1000 Scandinavian mercenaries on his side. This little army was attacked by Svyatopolk, who was in alliance with his wife's father, King Boleslav of Poland. Now we have seen that Svyatopolk had also allied himself to the powerful and numerous Pechenegs. In fact Yaroslav's little force was sandwiched in between two armies, both far more wealthy and numerous than his own—the Pechenegs to the east, the Poles to the west. Annihilation seemed certain; but at this point something happened which is unexplained in the *Povêst*, but of which the importance can hardly be overestimated. This was nothing less than a quarrel between Boleslav and Svyatopolk.

The quarrel seems to have arisen from a plot on the part of Svyatopolk to murder Boleslav and the Poles, who, after the recent defeat of Yaroslav, were actually ruling in Kiev. The plot was discovered, and Boleslav fled; but Svyatopolk and his Pecheneg allies were not strong enough without Polish support to withstand Yaroslav in the ensuing battle, and after a severe struggle Svyatopolk's forces were overcome, and Svyatopolk fled to Brest in Lithuania, where he subsequently perished. The account of the battle and of Svyatopolk's fate is among the most vivid and dramatic passages in the *Povêst*, and full of echoes of Norse skaldic poetry. Meanwhile Yaroslav made good his advantages by penetrating to Brest; but a new danger arose from Mstislav of Tmutorakan, who had collected a force of Khazars and Kasogs, and, taking advantage no doubt of the recent defeat of the Pechenegs, appeared with his allies as a claimant for the throne of Kiev.

Once more Yaroslav was in difficulties for men and money. Once more, we are told, while the men of Kiev successfully opposed the entry of Mstislav, Yaroslav, who was still in the north, returned to his old principality at Novgorod 'from where he sent overseas for Varangians'. His summons was answered. Hákon[1] came over with his Varangian followers. But the old story was repeated. The Varangians were overcome, and 'when Yaroslav saw that he was overpowered, he fled from the field

[1] It is interesting to note that the name Hákon is not Swedish, but Norwegian.

with Hákon…. Yaroslav arrived safely at Novgorod, but Hákon departed beyond the sea.' The description of this battle, and especially the ·picture of the blind Norse king Hákon, conspicuous in his gold-woven garment, are again redolent of Norse skaldic poetry, and more especially the *Hákonarmál* and the prose passages in Snorri's *Saga of Hákon the Good* in the *Heimskringla* which relate to the battle of Storth.[1] If space permitted it would have been profitable to have examined more fully the account of the Russian battle, and of the part played by King Hákon, here curiously represented as blind, yet as in the midst of the combatants in gold armour, and to have compared this Russian narrative with Snorri's account of the battle of Storth fought c. A.D. 960, in which an earlier King Hákon also fights in the midst of the battle, conspicuous in his golden helmet. The Norse saga is frankly based on contemporary Norse skaldic poetry. We are fortunate in possessing the text of the poem, which is known to have been composed by the skald Eyvindr Finsson, the grandnephew of King Hákon himself, who also personally took part in the battle, fighting at the king's side. The text of the *Povêst* is here so closely reminiscent of skaldic poetry, and even of this individual poem, that I find it impossible to avoid a suspicion that the author of the *Povêst*, or his informant, was acquainted with some version of the *Hákonarmál* or a similar skaldic poem composed on the same battle, and that he or his informant, perhaps another and later Norse skald, has adapted it to the later battle in which another and later Hákon took part.

I find it difficult to believe that a blind Norse king really fought in the midst of the Russian battle; but it is a very common motif in Norse sagas to find a blind man fighting in the midst of a battle and subsequently disappearing, as the blind Hákon is here hinted to have done. In Norse this blind belligerent invariably proves eventually to have been the god Óthinn. On such occasions he sometimes wears a slouch hat, but he is also represented as wearing

[1] The text of the Norse poem, together with a translation and an account of the battle which it celebrates, is given by N. Kershaw, *Anglo-Saxon and Norse Poems* (Cambridge, 1922), pp. 101 ff

a golden helmet, the *oegishjálmr*, and it is no doubt by an adroit skaldic hyperbole that King Hákon is thus, by his golden helmet, identified with the god to whose cult the Norwegian kings were especially devoted.

One curious detail of the Norse poem calls for comment. We are told in the *Saga of Hákon the Good*, in which the text of the *Hákonarmál* is quoted, that the poet Eyvindr, seeing that the king's golden helmet was rendering him conspicuous to his enemies, drew a hood over the helmet, whereupon one of the enemy cried loudly: 'Is the king of the Norwegians hiding, or has he fled? Where has his golden helmet vanished?' Is it possible that in this incident of the hood, which in itself suggests an attempt to reconcile the variant conceptions of Óthinn in his golden *oegishjálmr* and in his slouched hat which always falls low over his face, we also have the original detail which has been transformed in the Russian version into a picture of the blind king in his golden armour?

Now the Norse poem, the *Hákonarmál*, is itself a close and frank adaptation of an earlier poem known as the *Eiríksmál*, composed by an unknown skald on the death of King Hákon's predecessor on the Norwegian throne, King Eric (O.N. Eiríkr). The author of the *Hákonarmál*, Eyvindr Finsson, is known by the nickname *Skaldaspillir* (lit. 'Plagiarist'), in virtue of his practice of adapting the poems of his predecessors to contemporary events. His other chief poem, the *Háleygjatal*, which is preserved only in fragments, is just as evidently based on the *Ynglingatal* of the skald Thjó-thólfr of Hvín. It would be therefore in no way surprising to find some member of Yaroslav's Scandinavian following adapting the *Hákonarmál* to the later Hákon, and a paraphrase by the unknown and later *skaldaspillir* forming the basis of this passage in the *Povêst*. I have dwelt somewhat fully on this point because I am convinced that it would be possible to demonstrate the dependence of much of this part of the *Povêst* on contemporary poems—not narrative poems such as we find in the Norse *Elder Edda* and the Russian *byliny*, but short allusive poems like those of the Norse skalds, and passages in the Russian *Zadonshchina* and the *Slovo o Polku Igorevê*. Space will not permit me to go into the matter more fully here. It may, however, be pointed out in support of my suggestion that whenever in the *Povêst* the narrative is concerned in any way with the Scandinavians, the narrative at once becomes full and detailed, and is marked by terse and often sardonic wit, such as is the peculiar feature of the Norse sagas and Norse skaldic poetry, while in general the Russian relations with the Lithuanian peoples and with the Bulgarians and Greeks are related in bare annalistic form, a sure indication that no oral poems on these events current among the people in question were known to the chroniclers.

Ultimately a division was agreed upon between Yaroslav and Mstislav, and the latter reigned in Chernigov till his death in c. 1034, while Yaroslav ruled in Kiev. 'Thereafter', in the words of the *Povêst* (s.a. 1034–1036), 'Yaroslav took over all his power and was the sole ruler in the land of Rus.' The death of Mstislav seems to have weakened the Pecheneg command, for we hear of their final overthrow by Yaroslav in the following year.

Yaroslav no doubt realised that he owed his own success largely to Svyatopolk's political error in quarrelling with his powerful ally King Boleslav of Poland. Accordingly, he wisely established a union with Boleslav's successor Kazimir I of Poland, to whom he married his sister in 1043. The benefit of this union was felt later by Yaroslav's son Izyaslav, who had inherited the principate of Novgorod from his father, and who after his ejection from Kiev (whither he had fled after his defeat by the Polovtsy) fled to Kazimir for protection.

I have already referred to the contrast between the vivid picturesque style in which the *Povêst* relates Yaroslav's efforts in conjunction with the men of Novgorod and the Varangians against the Pechenegs and other eastern peoples, and that which recounts his activities against the Lithuanians. Thus in 1022 we have the laconic entry: 'Yaroslav came to Brest.' The statement undoubtedly bears some relationship to Svyatopolk's flight to Brest in 1019, and his death in the country beyond; but nothing more is told us of Yaroslav's purpose in this expedition three years later. Again, after his final accession to the throne of Kiev c. 1036, we find the equally curt entries in 1038: 'Yaroslav attacked the Yatvings'—the Yatvings are a Lithuanian tribe in the neighbourhood of Brest. In 1040: 'Yaroslav attacked the Lithuanians.' And again in 1041: 'Yaroslav attacked the Mazovians by boat.' The Mazovians are, of course, Poles. It would seem from these repeated attacks that the Lithuanians and Poles were in a position to offer a serious resistance to their eastern neighbours, and these attacks must have offered literary material as vivid and telling as those against the Pechenegs and Khazars; but absolutely nothing is told of the nature or even of the results of the expeditions. The conclusion is obvious enough. The writer of the *Povêst* is indebted to either saga or heroic poetry for everything relating to the struggle of the men of Novgorod and the Varangians against enemies coming from the east. No such material was available for attacks on Lithuania, in which, if we could make use of negative evidence, it would seem that the Novgorodians and Varangians did not in general take part.

The account which the *Povêst* gives of the last Greek expedition confirms this conclusion. This is the expedition sent by Yaroslav to attack the Greeks in 1043. The enterprise was entrusted to his son Vladimir, ruler of Novgorod, who is described by the Greek writer Skylitzes as a violent man and a great warrior,[1] and also to Vyshata, the *voevoda* of Kiev, himself the son of Ostromir of Novgorod (cf. p. 134 below). The expedition consisted of a fleet which is described by the contemporary Greek writer Psellos,[2] who was an eyewitness of the battle which followed, as exceedingly large; but according to Skylitzes it consisted of 'dugout canoes', though he also mentions that the expedition consisted of over 100,000 men—truly a strange flotilla! When the Russian fleet reached the Propontis it suffered a disastrous defeat at the hands of the Greeks. The defeat is attributed in the *Povêst*

[1] Cedrenus, Vol. II, Bonn, 1839, p. 551.
[2] See Michael Psellos, *Chronographie*, ed. and transl. by É. Renauld (Paris, 1928), p. 9.

to a violent storm, but there can be no doubt that the Russian expedition was no match for the Greeks under the command of the famous admiral, Michael Attaleiates, and they were further discomfited by the 'liquid fire' of which the Greeks made use.[1] Vladimir managed to escape to Russia, but Vyshata and the men who had been cast ashore were taken prisoners to Constantinople. Psellos describes the defeat as a terrible disaster for the Russians, and declares that the waves round the shore were red with blood,[2] while Skylitzes tells us that more than 15,000 Scandinavian bodies lay on the shores of the Bosphoros.[3]

The whole incident is described in the *Povêst* with great minuteness, which suggests the narrative of an eyewitness, written in a highly developed saga style. It is natural to suppose that on his return from Byzantium three years later Vyshata told the story to his son Yan, who recounted it in the best Novgorod saga style among the *mnoga slovesa* for which the *Povêst* is indebted to him. But the nature of the narrative suggests that it originated, not in a mere rambling reminiscence, but from a contemporary poem, such as Vyshata's *druzhina* may well have made on the heroic action of their leader. To this subject I shall return later.

We are fortunate in being able to supplement the entries in the *Povêst* for the reign of Yaroslav from both Norse and Greek sources, which are particularly rich for this period. Yaroslav is well known from Norse sources, no less than from Russian.[4] During the early part of his life, owing to his position as prince of Novgorod and his dependence on Scandinavian and Varangian support, Yaroslav represents a strong reaction against Vladimir's pro-Greek policy, and a return to the pro-Norse policy, which Vladimir seems to have abandoned. Yaroslav's pro-Scandinavian sympathies were no doubt fostered from his childhood, for his mother was the proud Swedish princess Ragnheithr of Polotsk,

---

[1] Cedrenus, *loc. cit.*
[2] Psellos, p. 11, footnote 2.
[3] Cedrenus, Vol. II, p. 553.
[4] See for fuller references an article by S. H. Cross, 'Yaroslav the Wise in Norse Tradition', in *Speculum*, Vol. IV (1929), pp. 177 ff.

who had been forced to marry Vladimir against her will.[1] This injury, sufficiently humiliating in itself for the haughty Scandinavian, must have been greatly accentuated by Vladimir's later marriage to the Greek princess Anna,[2] in addition to his tampering with the beautiful wife of his brother Yaropolk, herself also a Greek nun.[3] There can be no doubt that Ragnheithr would influence Yaroslav against his father and develop in him Scandinavian sympathies. This was doubtless the cause also of his refusing the tribute to Vladimir which we are told had always been paid by Novgorod.[4]

Yaroslav had married a Swedish wife, Ingigerthr, and he seems at all times to have depended largely on his Varangian guard, which we are told in the *Povêst* consisted of 1000 men. Their unruly conduct led the prince into difficulties with the men of Novgorod in early life, and it is very possible that the men of Novgorod resented the repeated tendency of the Varangians, like all mercenary soldiers, to hang back in moments of crisis if their remuneration was not to their liking. In the *Eymundartháttr*, a short Icelandic saga contained in the *Flateyjarbók*, we find repeated quarrels between Yaroslav and his champion and supporter Eymundr because the king will not, or cannot, pay him adequately, in consequence of which the Norseman constantly threatens to leave his service. Nothing of this is said in the *Povêst*; but the saga, despite the manifestly unhistorical character of much of its narrative, certainly lends support to the impression—clearly conveyed by the *Povêst*—that Yaroslav's Varangians were not whole-hearted in the struggle. This half-hearted support also accounts for Yaroslav's own readiness to flee to Sweden when things went adversely. It is in the light of the Norse evidence, which represents Yaroslav as niggardly and penurious, that we may explain the otherwise isolated and somewhat otiose entry in the *Povêst* to the effect that Mstislav was 'a

[1] Cross, s.a. 6486–6488 (A.D. 978–980).
[2] Cross, s.a. 6496 (A.D. 988).
[3] Cross, s.a. 6486–6488 (A.D. 978–980).
[4] Cross, s.a. 6520–6522 (A.D. 1012–1014).

great lover of his retainers, begrudging them neither treasure nor food nor drink'. And it is perhaps in contrast to the term 'crooked-shanks', with which Svyatopolk's general had taunted Yaroslav, that the *Povêst* observes as a kind of obituary notice, after recording his death s.a. 1034–1036, that the bold and heroic Mstislav was 'thick-set and red-faced, with large eyes, bold in battle, merciful, and a great lover of his retainers, begrudging them neither treasure nor food nor drink'. Such personal descriptions are not common in the *Povêst*. Curiously enough we get a similar miniature of Rostislav, son of Vladimir and grandson of Yaroslav, who was also prince of Tmutorakan; for again after narrating with great minuteness the circumstances of his death by poison at the hands of the Greeks, the chronicler adds (s.a. 1066), again as a kind of obituary notice: 'Rostislav was a man bold in war, fair of stature, and handsome of feature, and he was generous to the poor.' There can, I think, be little doubt that these obituary notices are derived from panegyric poetry composed and preserved by the *druzhinas*, and it is interesting to find the saga style again forcing itself in among the terse annals of the *Povêst* as soon as the chronicler turns his attention to the princes of Tmutorakan.

During the early part of the reign of Yaroslav, Greek interests are chiefly represented by Mstislav of Tmutorakan on the Taman Peninsula,[1] who succeeded in establishing himself on the throne of Chernigov and dividing 'the land of Russia' with Yaroslav his elder brother. On the other hand Yaroslav's dependence on his Varangians, and his close connections with Sweden, to which we have referred above, are persistently emphasised in both Scandinavian and Russian tradition. We may point also to the story of his summons of the blind Norse king Hákon to his aid in his struggle against Mstislav in 1024, and the prominent place which he assigned to the Varangians in the centre of his force in his fight against the Pechenegs in Kiev (s.a. 6542–6544, A.D. 1034–1036). We have seen also that Yaroslav was far-sighted enough

[1] We may refer especially to the entry which relates to his interment in the church which he had himself founded, s.a. 6542–6544 (A.D. 1034–1036).

to make peace with the Poles, whom his brother Svyatopolk had alienated, and that he cemented the alliance by marrying his sister to Kazimir. It was doubtless with the intention of creating an independent Russia that he finally launched an expedition against the Greeks in 1043. This, however, proved unsuccessful, and it was probably as a direct result of his defeat, and of the three years' sojourn of his *voevoda* Vyshata in Constantinople, that Yaroslav adopted and developed Greek culture and learning and became active in the building and endowment of churches and monasteries. It is to this period that Adam of Bremen refers when he speaks of Kiev as *aemula sceptri Constantinopolitani, clarissimum decus Graeciae*, 'vying with the power of Constantinople, and the most glorious jewel of Greece'.[1] There is nothing in the reigns of Vladimir's successors to suggest that they divested themselves of such dependence on 'Greece' as he himself may have had.

We shall see in the following chapter that the division of opinion and of political sympathies between what we may call the pro-Greek party on the one hand and the nationalist party on the other grew greater rather than less with time. In the reign of Yaroslav's successor Svyatopolk, who married a Greek wife, the anti-Greek feeling was inflamed by excessive donations to the Church at a time when the resources of Kiev were strained to the utmost by the attacks of the Polovtsy, the nomads who succeeded the Pechenegs on the Russian steppes in the latter half of the eleventh century. The enraged populace attacked all the foreign elements in Kiev, including the so-called 'Jews',[2] and clamoured for Vladimir, cousin of Svyatopolk and grandson of Yaroslav, to unite the princes and marshal the native elements, first against the Greek party, and then against the Polovtsy. I think that in this movement we can detect something more than a momentary feeling of irritation against the ecclesiastical party in Kiev itself. It seems more likely that the Russians realised that the arrival of the Polovtsy on the south

---

[1] *Gesta Hammaburgensis Ecclesiae Pontificum*, II, 19.
[2] Cf. however p. 129 below.

Russian steppes offered a golden opportunity to throw off the Greek suzerainty which seems to have been assumed by Vladimir I, and to divert the wealth of the Church to purchase immunity from the Polovtsy and so gain time for more final measures of independence. It is on some such basis that we can best explain the events in the *Povêst* which led to the call of Vladimir from Chernigov, the rapprochements and intermarriages which took place between the Russian and the Polovtsy leaders, and the proud assumption by Vladimir II of the title of Monomakh, which was actually the title of the Greek emperor Constantine.

These events will become clearer as we proceed.

Yaroslav was the first of the Russian rulers who can fairly be said to have held something of an international position among the reigning houses of the Europe of his time. He was evidently widely known outside his own country, both in oral poetry and saga and in diplomatic circles. He is the only Russian referred to in the *Older* or *Poetic Edda*, the most important early collection of Norse heroic and mythological poetry, where his name occurs under the form *Jarizleifr* in the poem known as the *Guthrúnarkvitha II* (*hin forna*), str. 20. His name figures more prominently than that of any other Russian in the Norse historical sagas.[1] One of his daughters was married to Harold Harthráthi, king of Norway, who had been for some years in his service.

Yaroslav was keenly awake to the diplomatic advantages of intermarriage with the reigning houses in the west. He married another of his daughters to Henry I, king of France, and yet another to Andrew, king of Hungary. Russia was beginning to play her part in international politics. Progress at home kept pace, and Yaroslav is said to have been responsible for the promulga-

[1] I take occasion to refer again here to the interesting and suggestive article by S. H. Cross on 'Yaroslav the Wise in Norse Tradition' (*Speculum*, Vol. IV, 1929, p. 177), where the Norse traditions relating to Yaroslav are examined in considerable detail—a most welcome piece of work, and the beginning of better things for the study of the relations between Scandinavia and Russia in early times. Further Norse references to Yaroslav could be added to those enumerated by Cross.

tion of the earliest Russian code of written laws, the famous *Russkaya Pravda.*

The writer of the *Povêst* has nothing but praise for Yaroslav owing to his munificence to the Church and his important contributions to culture generally; but it is easy to see that in native tradition Yaroslav was unpopular, and that his unpopularity was due to his Scandinavian allies and connections. It is especially interesting therefore to find that this same unpopularity clings to him also in Norse tradition, though the reason there assigned is stinginess. The same cause must lie behind both traditions. It would seem likely that Yaroslav did not commend himself to his *voevodas,* who did not supply him with enough money. Perhaps they found the Varangian exactions too heavy in addition to his extensive donations to the Church. But the chief cause is doubtless more deep-seated. The *voevodas,* despite Vyshata's part in the expedition of 1043, were consistently pro-Greek in their sympathies; and in this they were probably merely continuing a traditional attitude and policy adopted long before the appearance of the Scandinavians on Russian soil. Yaroslav's Scandinavian policy was disliked, and it was only after his final crushing defeat at the hands of the Greeks and his consequent adoption of Greek culture that he commended himself to the chronicler.

I am inclined to regard this disastrous expedition of Yaroslav's as of more far-reaching consequences than has generally been supposed, and as the death blow to Scandinavian hopes in the near east. In particular Vasiliev[1] fails to realise its relationship to Yaroslav's general policy, its significance as the crisis and the conclusion of Russo-Greek relations in the early period of Russian history. It is clear both from the size of the fleet, which is emphasised by Psellos, and also from its place in the chronology of Yaroslav's alliances and conquests, that it was the supreme effort of his reign, and one towards which his previous efforts had been mainly directed. It is clear, moreover, from Greek sources, that he had made himself well acquainted with political

---

[1] See the brief paragraph devoted to this expedition in his *Histoire de l'Empire Byzantin,* Vol. I, p. 428.

events in the Greek empire, and that he well knew the right moment at which to strike. The failure of this supreme effort was the death blow to the Viking Age in the East. With the failure of Yaroslav's hopes, the hopes of the Norsemen in the East also perished. We have seen that the expedition was headed by leaders of Novgorod interests, and we have seen that Yaroslav depended in all his enterprises principally on Scandinavian troops. We have also seen (p. 105 above) that according to Skylitzes more than 15,000 Scandinavian bodies lay on the shores of the Bosphoros after the battle. The same writer tells us that on this same tragic shore the Greeks took innumerable prisoners and cut off their right hands. These thousands of human hands were afterwards exposed on the ramparts of the capital.

Why? I suggest that it was a natural precaution on the part of the Greeks to preclude further attacks from the Varangians, whose long swords they knew only too well. And at the same time it was a signal of their final triumph over their old enemy. The *Povêst* makes mention only of the blinding of the prisoners. But it also tells us the interesting fact that the *voevoda* Vyshata did not return to Russia with Vladimir. He remained behind with the troops on the shore; but he did not suffer their fate. He was taken to Byzantium, but there is no suggestion that he suffered any punishment, and after three years he returned to Kiev, where he and his sons, Yan and Putyata, became the leading representatives of Greek culture and interests. I am not without a suspicion that Vyshata, following the policy of most of the other *voevodas*, sacrificed the Varangians to the Greeks in this battle, and once for all forced the prince of Kiev to submit to their ancient friend, or perhaps suzerain, the Greek emperor. Be that as it may, and whatever the part played by Vyshata, the outstanding result of the battle is the total disappearance of the Varangians at this point from the pages of Russian history.

CHAPTER VII

VOEVODA AND KORMILETS

There are numerous signs throughout the reigns of Yaroslav and his successors that the national consciousness of the native populations was by no means overwhelmed by the Scandinavian princes. We have seen the populations of both Novgorod and Kiev forming themselves into powerful bodies which were in a position to take matters into their own hands when they chose, and to dictate their own terms to their princes, even to coerce the princes to their own will. This popular consciousness is seen also in the heathen reactions which take place from time to time, and show themselves in sudden and apparently unaccountable manifestations of Finnish shamanism. Indeed it is in the entries in the *Povêst* which recount these reactions, or rather in the measures taken by the Christian princes to stamp them out, that we can glean some idea of heathen Russia which, however slight, is yet a more genuine tradition than that of Vladimir's idols.

These indications of religious reaction are generally associated with popular discontent consequent upon times of famine. Thus in 6532 (1024) we are told that magicians (*volsvi*) came to Suzdal, killing old people by *naushchenie* ('teaching' or 'instigation') and *bêsovanie* ('devilry'), declaring that 'the harvest is being held back'; but Yaroslav seized some and dispersed the rest. The chronicler adds that he then returned to Novgorod and sent overseas for Varangians, for he was at the height of his struggle against Mstislav, and the fact that he should pay attention to the Suzdal shamans in such a crisis shows the importance which he attached to their influence, and their close association with the political situation. Nearly fifty years later, in 6579 (1071), we learn that during the inroads of the Polovtsy, which, as we know from other sources, precluded agriculture around Kiev, which supplied the citizens with food, a 'magician inspired by the devil' (*volkhv prêlshchen bêsom*) appeared in Kiev, prophesying by concrete imagery what appear to be certain political and international changes. It is significant that immediately after this entry we are told that there was famine in the district of Rostov, and, simultaneously, two wizards (*dva volkhva*) came from Yaroslav on the Volga, declaring that the famine was caused by certain women whom they accused of affecting the grain, fish and furs, and as they stabbed the women in the back they feigned to draw these commodities out of them—an interesting piece of Finnish conjuring. They marched to Bêlo-ozero accompanied by some three hundred men, and the affair was regarded as of enough importance for representations to be made to Yan, the son of Vyshata, the *voevoda* of Kiev, who happened to be collecting tribute in the neighbourhood. The encounter between Yan and the wizards is extremely interesting in itself, but is too long to give here. It is related with relish and crude humour, but it is a painful story, and one which reflects more credit on the victims than on the Christian official of the court of Kiev. At the same time the minute detail with which the dialogue and the doctrines of the *volkhva* are related, and for which the chronicler is undoubtedly indebted to Yan, does credit to the wide intellectual curiosity of Yan himself, and shows that the mental activity of his family was not restricted even to Greek learning and native oral tradition.

It will be profitable at this moment to pause and consider the part played by the *voevodas* in the history of the period. The majority of these bear Slavonic names, all are men of very considerable authority, and in at least some important families the office is hereditary. We have seen Dobrynya and Blud, the *voevodas* of Novgorod and Kiev respectively, under first Yaropolk and then Vladimir, and we have watched them making and unmaking their puppet princes at pleasure. Dobrynya's son Constantine was *posadnik* of Novgorod when Yaroslav planned to flee overseas after his defeat by Boleslav, king of Poland; but with a high hand Constantine destroyed the boats and forced

Yaroslav to renew the struggle.[1] The same technique had been
adopted earlier by Yaroslav's Novgorod supporters when he
crossed the Dnêpr to attack his brother Svyatopolk in his struggle
for Kiev on Vladimir's death; for we are told that when Yaroslav
had crossed the river his forces disembarked on the shore and
pushed the boats out from the bank.[2] Probably, therefore,
Constantine's hand is to be traced in this drastic and autocratic
act also. During the struggle with Boleslav and Svyatopolk
which took place in the intervening period, however, Yaroslav's
voevoda was a certain Budy, who is also described as his *kormilets*,
and who seems to have been equally uncompromising in his
attitude to Boleslav, threatening to 'pierce his fat belly with a
pike'.[3] Many years later,[4] however, when Yaroslav sent his son
Vladimir on an expedition against the Greeks, we are told that
he assigned the *voevodstvo* to Vyshata, while at the same time a
certain Ivan Tvorimirovich is described as the *voevoda* who,
when the expedition was overtaken by a storm, saved Vladimir
from drowning by taking him into his boat. The behaviour of
Vyshata on this occasion is at once heroic and democratic, in
striking contrast to that of the prince. For Vladimir, after fighting a covering action with the pursuing Greek fleet, returned
home, abandoning the 6000 soldiers and Vyshata's *druzhina* who
had been cast on shore. Vyshata, however, disembarked to join
them, remarking: 'If I live it will be with the soldiers, and if I
perish it will be with my *druzhina*.' But he and his party were
captured by the Greeks, and he remained a prisoner in Byzantium for three years before he was released and allowed to
return to Russia.

The position of *voevoda* is hereditary in the families of Dobrynya
and Vyshata, and it can be shown (pp. 134 f. below) that while the
former is of princely rank, the latter certainly belongs to one of
the most important families in Russia. Sveinald, the *voevoda* first
of Igor, then of Svyatoslav, and finally of Yaropolk, must also
have been of high, if not of princely rank. The equipment of his

---

[1] *Povêst*, s.a. 6526 (A.D. 1018).   [2] *Ib*. s.a. 6524 (A.D. 1016).
[3] *Ib*. s.a. 6526 (A.D. 1018).   [4] *Ib*. s.a. 6551 (A.D. 1043).

followers is said to be superior to, and more gorgeous than that of Igor's own men (s.a. 945). While Oleg, Yaropolk's brother, was ruling the Drevlians in the city of Vruchi, he chanced while out hunting to meet Lyut, Sveinald's son, who was also hunting in the same forest, and Oleg killed Lyut, obviously regarding his act as one of defiance. Can Lyut's arrogance have been inspired by a desire to assert an ancient territorial right? Oleg's own act suggests that Lyut was a person of importance, for the chronicler informs us in detail that he carefully enquired who Lyut was, and on learning that he was Sveinald's son, he 'rode up and killed him'. What follows is equally significant; for we are told that Sveinald actually induced Yaropolk to kill his own brother, Oleg, in vengeance for Lyut, an act which is surely highly significant of the estimation in which the families of the *voevodas* were held by the descendants of Rurik. It is difficult to believe that Yaropolk would have taken such extreme vengeance for anyone of less than princely rank, and unless he were compelled by superior force.

The question arises, did the title *voevoda* signify something in the nature of a ruler at this time in Russia, as in Rumania in the sixteenth and seventeenth centuries?[1] We may note in passing that in the early document relating to the Khazars, to which we have frequently referred, it is stated that 'there was no king in the land of Khazaria. Only him who won victories in the battle they would appoint over them as general of the army.'[2] It is not impossible, therefore, that the institution of the *voevoda* may have been borrowed by the Slavs of the Dnêpr from the Khazars in

---

[1] The original meaning of the term was, of course, 'leader of the army' (Old Slavonic *voin*, pl. *voi*, 'soldiers', *voditi*, 'to lead'). But the Roumanian princes Michael the Brave who came to the throne of Wallachia in 1593, and Matthew Bassarab who ruled Wallachia from 1633 to 1654, are both described by the term *vaivoda* (*voivoda*) (see the two portraits published by the Roumanian Government from historical MSS. and reproduced by W. Miller in *The Balkans* (London, 1896), pp. 50, 65).

[2] See 'An Unknown Khazar Document', *ed. cit.*, p. 213. Cf. further what Mas'udi says (ch. 17) of the relationship of the khagan of the Khazars to the king.

the ninth century. It may be pointed out that in the early
occurrence of the office during the rule of Olga, Sveinald is
described as *voevoda* of the child Svyatoslav, while Asmund is
his *kormilets*, as I have explained below. The twofold office at
this early date would accord well with the theory that one represented the traditional local executive officer, the other the
intrusive Norse. In any case there can be no doubt that the
voevodas constitute the most solid element in the early Russian
aristocracy. Despite the chronicler's obvious desire to exalt the
house of Rurik as the founders of the Church and patrons of
Greek learning, we cannot fail to read between the lines that
politically Vladimir I, Yaroslav, and perhaps even Monomakh
himself, were little more than puppets in the hands of these
native king-makers. Throughout the pages of the chronicle we
see that it is the *voevodas* from father to son who govern the course
of events, who control the careers of the princes, who support
them morally and materially in war and in peace, who guard
their persons, and protect their honour and that of the nation in
moments of danger and vacillation, and who cast in their lot
with the soldiery like the heroic princes of old.

An interesting question which we cannot afford to neglect is
that of the more immediate relationship of the *voevoda* to the
kormilets. We have seen that Yaroslav's *voevoda* Budy is said to
have been also his *kormilets*. We are also told that while the child
Svyatoslav was in Kiev with his mother Olga, his *kormilets* was
a certain Asmund, while the *voevoda* was in this case a different
person, namely one Sveinald, the father of two sons Mstikha and
Lyut. Asmund and Sveinald are both Norse names, but Mstikha
and Lyut are Slavonic. The wording of the annals[1] suggests that
both the persons and the functions of Asmund and Sveinald were
well known to tradition; and Asmund as *kormilets* to the child
Svyatoslav was fulfilling the same function as Oleg to the infant
Igor, whom, as we have seen, Rurik left in Oleg's charge to be
brought up because he was very young (cf. p. 21 above).

The word *kormilets* means literally 'one who feeds', 'pro-

[1] *Povêst*, s.a. 6453 (A.D. 945), 6482–6483 (A.D. 974–975).

visor';[1] but it is clear from the position of Oleg and Asmund that much more is implied than the mere supply of food. The *kormilets* was undoubtedly responsible for the general well-being and up-bringing of the young prince in question, and seems to have combined the functions of tutor with those of provisor. The office seems to correspond exactly to that of the Norse *fóstri* of which the word *kormilets* is an exact translation, and it is in exactly the sense of the Norse *fóstri* that the word *kormilets* appears to have been used in early times in Russia. The custom of 'foster-age', that is, of entrusting a boy to someone else, generally a friend or relative, to bring up, figures both in early Norse runic inscriptions and in early Norse[2] and early Irish literature, and was probably practised in both Scandinavia and Ireland. It would be interesting to know whether the custom prevailed also among the Slavonic peoples. Here we may note that the three people who stand in this position to the princes all have Norse names, while the *voevodas* generally have Slavonic ones, though, as we have seen, Yaroslav's *kormilets* is said to have been also his *voevoda*.

The evidence would seem to suggest that the *voevodas* with their Slavonic names and titles, their hereditary rights and high, even princely rank, their paramount prestige and heroic ideals, were, in fact, the native Russian hereditary aristocracy. The evidence suggests further that this native Russian aristocracy was not abolished or even displaced by the coming of the Norse rulers. On the contrary, the Norse rulers were largely dependent on them, not only for their position, but also for their mainten-ance and organisation. This question of maintenance was by no means an academic one, as we have seen in the case of Yaroslav, under whom the question of supplies and finance seems to have assumed an acute form. The humorous anecdote of the wooden

[1] A number of quotations illustrating the use of this word from Russian literary sources will be found *s.v.* in the *Slovar Russkago Yazika*, published by the Russian Imperial Academy, St Petersburg, 1895–1907.

[2] An interesting discussion of the picture of supernatural fosterage from the mythical sagas, as distinct from the historical references, is given by H. R. Ellis in a paper entitled 'Fosterage by Giants in Old Norse Sagas', in *Medium Ævum*, Vol. x (1942), pp. 70ff.

spoons suggests that even Vladimir I may have been similarly embarrassed. In an agricultural country like Russia only an ancient traditional territorial organisation could have supported a régime like that of the merchant princes of the Dnêpr. This paramount question of agriculture is repeatedly stressed in the *Povêst*. It was fully realised also by all the steppe nomads, who knew that they had only to obstruct agriculture in the environs of the Dnêpr cities and the citizens would be forced to capitulate. Pechenegs, Khazars, Polovtsy all economised men and fighting power by making the most of this simple technique. Without stable agricultural conditions the Scandinavian kingdom of the Dnêpr could not have subsisted a year;[1] but manifestly they themselves could not have organised Russian local agriculture. The commissariat of the nation could only have been carried out by the local Russian aristocracy with the local Russian peasantry behind them.

How did the *voevodas* come to occupy this position in regard to the Scandinavian princes? Perhaps it would be more natural to ask: How did the Scandinavian princes attain their high authority and prestige under such conditions? In what did their importance primarily lie for early Russia? How did they come to rule?

Perhaps the most natural explanation, after all, is the one given by the *Povêst* itself. According to its testimony, shortly after the middle of the ninth century, and immediately upon the downfall of the Bulgarian empire at the hands of the Greeks, the 'Varangians' imposed tribute on certain tribes living around the head waters of the Volga and the Dnêpr; that is to say on the principal watershed of northern Russia. This appears to have been a short-lived rule, if the chronology of the *Povêst* is to be relied on, for a year or two later we are told that the tributaries threw off the Varangian yoke and drove them overseas, only to find themselves unable to rule alone, in spite of the fact that they were avowedly rich and prosperous. The reason of their failure is also made clear

[1] We know from the insertion of Ohthere's voyage to Bjarmaland in King Alfred's translation of Orosius that agriculture was also practised in the north in the ninth century.

in the *Povêst*, for we are told at the same time that the Khazars imposed tribute on the Polians (that is to say, on the Russians in the neighbourhood of Kiev), on the Severians, and on some other northern tribes as well. The downfall of the Bulgarian empire had, in fact, laid the southern steppes completely open to Khazar penetration, and as we have seen, the Greeks found it their best policy to support them as a buffer state between the Greek world and the Varangian and Pecheneg menace. Accordingly the Slavs, so says the *Povêst*, sent invitations to three Scandinavian brothers, known as Varangian 'Rus', to come and rule over them, and Rurik with his brothers, Sineus and Truvor, came and settled in the northern lakes; and after the death of Sineus and Truvor Rurik assumed sole authority in the north and settled Varangian colonies in Polotsk, Rostov and Bêlo-ozero, etc.

There is nothing in this account which is at variance with later evidence, whether literary or archaeological. We know that the Scandinavians who settled in Russia were great traders, and that the more enterprising of them were also capable military leaders. We have also seen reason to believe that there were wealthy communities in Russia and that agriculture was extensively practised then as now. We read constantly in the Icelandic sagas of Scandinavian raids on Russia. On the other hand, the annals of the *Povêst* represent the country as constantly subject to inroads from the east from the Turkish peoples of the steppe. Not infrequently they were simultaneously subject to attacks from the west, especially from the Poles. In such circumstances it would be in no way surprising if the Slavs should invite their active and enterprising military neighbours to assist them as mercenaries, and that they should eventually come to employ them perforce as permanent garrisons with royal privileges and powers to protect them against the foes who threatened to annihilate them from east and west. Some such situation would best account for the attitude of the *voevodas* to the descendants of Rurik. It would account for their insistence that the princes should fight and lead their followers in battle, and it would also account for Yaroslav's lack of funds, and for the Scandinavian tradition of his stinginess (cf. p. 106 above).

CHAPTER VIII

VLADIMIR MONOMAKH

The disunion among the princes consequent upon the death of Yaroslav in 1054 was a signal for the Turkish nomads to make another incursion into the west. The Pechenegs were succeeded, shortly after Yaroslav's death, by another Turkish nomadic people from the steppe, known in Russian sources as Polovtsy, and to classical writers as Cumani. Their Turkish name is Kipchak. Three of Yaroslav's sons, including Izyaslav, who had been installed by Yaroslav as his successor in Novgorod, fought a battle outside Kiev against the Polovtsy by night in 1068, but were defeated and fled, leaving the people of Kiev a prey to their enemy. What follows is extremely significant in its bearing on the problem of the relationship of the descendants of Rurik with the *voevodas* and with the native Slavonic population. On this occasion, as on the occasion of Yaroslav's defeat at the hands of the Pechenegs in the neighbourhood of Kiev, the people of Kiev rallied, and determined to offer further resistance to the nomads.

To this end they held an assembly in the square and sent an appeal to Izyaslav: 'The Polovtsy have spread over the country; O Prince, give us arms and horses, that we may offer them combat once more.'

But Izyaslav turned a deaf ear to their appeal, as Yaroslav had done before, and perhaps for the same reason. The wording of the appeal is significant as indicating once more that the native population regarded the sons of Rurik and the Varangians as something in the nature of a garrison and a professional army. It is not impossible that the Varangians had prohibited the people of Kiev from bearing arms, and that the latter were in consequence somewhat in the position of the Armenians among the Turks before the War of 1914–18. It is interesting to note, however, that when the request of the people of Kiev was disregarded by Izyaslav, their displeasure was directed, not so much against Izyaslav himself, as against Constantine Kosnyachek, his *voevoda*.

The details of Izyaslav's struggle with the citizens, his flight to Poland, his treachery against his allies, and his final ascent to the throne need not concern us here. But it is a striking fact that at this point, as we come into contact with the personnel of Novgorod in its prince and *posadnik*, or 'governor', we also enter simultaneously into the same type of vivid and detailed narrative which we have previously found in a similar milieu. The account of Izyaslav's struggle with the citizens is a masterly little vignette, despite the fact that the same events are related twice with slight variants. We should have been tempted to suspect that we had before us in this scene the account of an eyewitness were it not for the fact that the repetition and variants make it clear that artistic narratives in the form of oral records are being paraphrased by the chronicler, and welded together by a hand not completely skilled.

Izyaslav was succeeded in 1078 by another of Yaroslav's sons, Vsevolod,[1] who, like his father and his brother Izyaslav,[2] favoured the Greek Church and Greek culture. He is mentioned as taking a prominent part in the translation of the saints, Boris and Gleb. He married a Greek princess, and made his own daughter Yanka a nun, and later sent her to Greece. The chronicler tells us that Vsevolod had loved God from his youth up, and showed honour to the clergy, and that he was especially devoted to all monks, endowing them heavily. But already before his death, which took place in A.D. 1093, we note signs of discontent among the people. He was not in close touch with his *druzhina*, and the people could not obtain justice. Throughout his reign the defence of the kingdom against aggression from every side seems to have been entrusted to his son Vladimir, who was later to become the great Monomakh.

On the death of Vsevolod, his son Vladimir, later Monomakh,

---

[1] His name occurs in Norse sagas as *Vissivaldr*.

[2] He is the founder of the great Pecherski Monastery in Kiev.

was in Kiev on a visit to his father's death-bed, and he could undoubtedly have ascended the throne in succession to his father; but, in the words of the chronicler: 'Vladimir reflected that if he succeeded immediately to the throne of his father, he would become involved in hostilities with Svyatopolk, because the throne of Kiev belonged to that prince's father. After thus taking thought he summoned Svyatopolk from Turov... Svyatopolk arrived in Kiev.... The inhabitants of Kiev went forth to meet him and offer him homage, and welcomed him joyously.'

At this point the Polovtsy, learning of the death of Vsevolod, and no doubt counting on a period of dissension among the Russian princes during a probable interregnum, seized the opportunity to make an attack on the kingdom of Kiev, but sent overtures for peace, probably expecting a heavy indemnity. Svyatopolk rashly, and without consulting the other princes who were in alliance with him, seized the Polovtsy envoys and cast them into prison. The Polovtsy, of course, at once declared war, whereupon Svyatopolk, 'being', we are told, 'desirous of peace, released the envoys'. This incident at the opening of his reign is typical of this courageous and well-intentioned but injudicious prince. His rash act opened the flood-gates of war on his capital before the Russian princes were in a position to stem it, and a period of stormy councils among the princes followed before any settled policy, whether of open hostilities against the Polovtsy, or of temporising, could be agreed upon. Meanwhile the Polovtsy, who were not particularly anxious for peace, continued their attacks against the city. Svyatopolk was anxious to fling himself upon the nomads with his force, hardly more than a *druzhina*, of 800 men: but the wiser heads within the city pointed out that even if he had 8000 men it would be an insufficient force for the present needs, and advised sending for his cousin Vladimir for aid.

Vladimir came. He first made a firm alliance with Svyatopolk against the aggressors, and then turned to attack the Polovtsy. But the first attempt was premature, as Vladimir himself had foreseen. He had indeed counselled his cousin to make peace, but was overborne, and a disastrous series of battles followed, in which the young prince Rostislav perished and Svyatopolk and Vladimir hardly escaped with their lives. In the meantime the cousins Svyatopolk and Vladimir were bending all their efforts to form an alliance on wider lines among the Russian princes; but their task was not easy, as there was obviously no spirit of nationalism whatever among the descendants of Rurik as a whole, and it was by no means rare to find the princes even acting in concert with their enemies, whether openly, like David, who left Novgorod at this period of crisis and settled at Smolensk among the Poles, or like Oleg, the hereditary prince of Chernigov, who dissembled friendship with the allied princes while virtually aiding the cause of the Polovtsy themselves, with whom he was clearly acting in conjunction. Indeed the chronicler tells us roundly that Oleg had himself inspired their raids on this and on previous occasions.

In 1094 Svyatopolk made a peace with the Polovtsy, cementing the alliance by marrying the daughter of their leader. His name is generally given in Russian records as Tugorkan, or Tugortkan, but this seems to be equivalent to Tugur Khan, and it always appears in the Russian oral narratives as Tugorín, to which is generally added the nickname Zmêevich, 'Dragon's son'. Vladimir also married his son Andrey to Tugur's granddaughter; but these marriages did not deter Tugur from further incursions, and there are some ugly stories of treachery on the part of the Russian princes themselves against their Polovtsy guests. These stories can hardly be trusted in the form in which they have come down to us, but it is not impossible that some genuine tradition of treachery may lie behind the saga material on which these entries are based.

We have already seen Vladimir voluntarily handing over Kiev to his cousin Svyatopolk as a part of his constructive policy of peace and alliance among the Russian princes. His next step is to hand over the city of Chernigov, to which he had retired on relinquishing Kiev, and which was probably the richest city in the valley of the Dnêpr at this time, to the faithless Oleg, in the hope of rallying him and his followers to the Russian standard. Vladimir himself now withdrew to Pereyaslavl. Here we are told the Polovtsy Itlar and Kytan came in 1095 to sue for peace.

The *Povêst* relates that Vladimir killed both Kytan and Itlar by treachery, while they were his guests and under his safe-conduct, and even after he had given them his son as a hostage. The story is related with picturesque and circumstantial detail, and both the manner of the murder of the Polovtsy leaders and the manner in which it is related bear a close resemblance to many a Norse saga, and have probably lost nothing in their transmission from some form of oral *slava* or paean composed to celebrate the event,[1] despite the fact that these events took place less than twenty years before the *Povêst* was written. It is even possible that some of the circumstances may be the conventional stock property of such stories. Itlar and his companions are said to have been murdered in a heated room in which they were dressing in the early morning, and which is clearly the Russian steam bath; and murder in the bath is not rare among the motifs of oral saga. Moreover, the chronicler is at pains to assure us that at first Vladimir was unwilling to do the deed, urging that it was 'unthinkable', in view of the pledges of safety which had been given to the Polovtsy. Nevertheless the actual effect of the manœuvre was to divide the Polovtsy forces and to put a large section of them out of action just at the time when the whole fate of the 'Rus' was hanging in the balance, and the story bears the stamp of strategy which is in accord with Vladimir's general policy in dealing with an enemy so much superior in numbers.

Before leaving this curious story, it is interesting to look at the names of the men to whom Vladimir is said to have entrusted the execution of his commissions. The treacherous invitation to Itlar to come to visit Vladimir is said to have been conveyed to

---

[1] Such *slovesa*, short oral poetical prose accounts, partly narrative, partly commentary, continued to be composed in Russia on contemporary events as late as the seventeenth century, and served, by passing from place to place, to circulate news like a modern newspaper.

him by Vladimir's servant, Bandyuk, which should more correctly be written Ban Dyuk. The term *Ban* is used as a title among the Yugoslavs, and generally refers to a governor of a province or town, such as Zara, while in the Russian *byliny* Dyuk is the name of a prince of Galicia. The instigator of the whole piece of treachery is said to bear the name Ratibor. Now this name is a compound of two Norse words *rath*, 'counsel', and *bera*, 'to bring',[1] and it simply means 'counsellor', though it also implies, in view of its etymology, that the counsellor in question was a man of Scandinavian extraction. His function in this instance recalls that of Bikki, the well-known 'evil counsellor' at the court of Ermenric in Teutonic heroic story. The actual murder of Itlar is said to have been performed by Ratibor's son Olbeg, who shot him through the heart with his bow and arrow. The name Olbeg is unknown to me; but the choice of bow and arrow to shoot a man at such close quarters—Olbeg is said to shoot Itlar through a hole in the roof of the heated room in which he is dressing—certainly suggests that Olbeg was one of the nomads. I have thought it worth while to point out that none of the people concerned appear to be Slavs, and it is interesting to notice the extremely mixed elements which are to be found in Russian politics during the Polovtsy crisis. A full and careful study of the proper names which occur in the *Povêst* would undoubtedly throw a flood of light on the internal and external politics of the period, and also on the sources and the milieu from which the chronicler has derived his information, and would be of great assistance to us in the difficult task of assessing the relative reliability of the various entries. In the present story it is to be greatly doubted if any of the proper names can be trusted, unless it is that of Slavyata, who is said to have been responsible for the death of Kytan; and that of Svyatoslav, Vladimir's son, who is said to have been given as a hostage to his guests.

After the death of their leaders at Pereyaslavl, the Polovtsy camp fell an easy prey to Vladimir and Svyatopolk, who, emboldened by their success, again made efforts to compel Oleg and

[1] Cf. A.S. *rædbora*, 'counsellor'.

David to join in what seems to have been a well-planned attempt to cut off the Polovtsy in the south from their allies in the north. Oleg temporised, but was ultimately forced to join the alliance in the following year, though David resisted and barricaded himself in Smolensk. Meanwhile, in what may well have been a punitive expedition, the Polovtsy leaders, Bonyak and Kurya, besieged Kiev and Pereyaslavl respectively, burning and pillaging apparently without resistance. Almost immediately, and doubtless encouraged by the success of Bonyak and Kurya, Tugur led an army to besiege Pereyaslavl. Undeterred by close ties of marriage, Svyatopolk, together with Vladimir, marched against Tugur. The Polovtsy were surprised and defeated. Many of their princes were slain, and both Tugur and his son were killed in the ensuing battle. Tugur's body was discovered next morning, and Svyatoslav gave orders that it should be brought to Kiev and buried near Berestovoye.

The success of Svyatopolk and Vladimir against the Polovtsy on the Dnêpr was undoubtedly materially assisted by a simultaneous expedition organised by Mstislav Vladimirovich, Monomakh's son, in the north against those princes who refused to join the alliance of the southern princes. The attack of Tugur has generally been regarded as a raid; but the conduct of the princes Oleg and Yaroslav, both at this time and in previous years, suggests that concerted action was planned between them and the main body of the Polovtsy of the south, and that the simultaneous action of Mstislav of Novgorod in the north, and of his *voevoda* Dobrynya Raguelovich, with that of Svyatopolk and Vladimir Monomakh on the southern Dnêpr was carefully planned in order to cut off the Polovtsy forces from their northern allies. Thanks to the vigorous and successful offensive of Dobrynya, backed by the able support of Mstislav, and thanks also, we are told, to the prayers of the holy bishop Nikita of Novgorod, this plan was completely successful. The check given by Dobrynya and Mstislav, justly called 'the Brave', to the movements of the northern princes at the very moment when the southern Polovtsy were attacking the cities of the Dnêpr almost certainly accounts for the disaster suffered by the Polovtsy at Pereyaslavl and the death of Tugur Khan.

The defeat of Tugur was not the end of the Polovtsy, but it was the harbinger of the end. David from Smolensk succeeded in making common cause with Bonyak, and Svyatopolk called in Hungarian reinforcements to resist them; but the Hungarians were defeated and Mstislav himself was killed by a chance arrow. His retainers are reported to have suppressed the news of his death for three days, as the death of Vladimir I was kept secret at an earlier date. His death was avenged by Svyatopolk's *voevoda* Putyata, and in 1100 we have the important entry: 'This year the cousins Svyatopolk, Vladimir, David and Oleg concluded peace among themselves', while immediately afterwards we read proposals of peace from the Polovtsy leaders which were accepted by the Russian princes. The growing prestige of Svyatopolk consequent upon his military successes, and perhaps of the alliance among the princes also consequent upon these successes, is perhaps to be seen in the marriage of Svyatopolk's daughter Sbyslava to King Boleslav of Poland in the following year, to be followed two years later by the marriage of another daughter Predslava to the son of the king of Hungary.

In 1103 [1] we are told impressively by the chronicler that God inspired a noble project in the hearts of the cousins Svyatopolk and Vladimir. This was nothing less than an offensive operation on the grand scale against the main body of the Polovtsy forces. The deliberations of the war council are reported to us in detail. The supporters of Svyatopolk are represented to us as counselling delay, on the ground that to open hostilities in the spring would ruin the peasants and their fields, in reply to which Vladimir is represented as pointing out that to delay till the time of ploughing would mean that the Polovtsy would come and massacre the harvester and carry off his horse, his wife and family and all his property. Svyatopolk declared himself for final supremacy against the nomad. Oleg as before stood back.

[1] According to the Hypatian text of the *Povêst* the events which follow took place in 1111.

The Russian army lost no time, but set off at once by horse and boat till they arrived below the Cataracts, and then mounted and rode for four days till they reached a place referred to in the chronicle as Suten. Here they were met by the Polovtsy forces, led by the redoubtable Altun Apa, who had led them to victory in their earlier attack, in company with Bonyak, against the Hungarian allies of Svyatopolk. The Polovtsy troops seem to have been taken by surprise by the precipitate attack of the Russians, and were completely defeated. Altun Apa was slain, and along with him twenty Polovtsy princes. The Polovtsy chief, whose name is given as Beldyuz, was taken prisoner, and offered a rich ransom for himself. Svyatopolk declined to decide the matter and sent him to Vladimir, who directed that he should be executed, and he is said to have been instantly cut to pieces. The Russians returned to their homes, laden with booty from the Polovtsy camp, 'carrying great spoil and a great victory won'.

In 1106 we hear of another raid by the Polovtsy which is said to have been driven off by Yan, the son of Vyshata, and his brother Putyata, and by Ivan the Khazar. The combination is significant, as we shall see. Again in the following year another raid by Bonyak is reported as having been made against Pereyaslavl, while the same year Bonyak and Sharu Khan the Old laid siege to Lyubny. The alliance of Russian princes quickly put them to flight, slaying Bonyak's brother, while Sharu Khan barely escaped with his life, and once more the Russians returned home with great victory. A few months later peace was once more cemented between the Russian princes and the nomads by means of marriages, Vladimir taking one daughter of Ay Apa[1] to be the wife of Prince Yury,[2] while Oleg took another daughter of Ay Apa as a wife for his son.

[1] This is probably a relative of Altun or Altyn Apa. *Altyn* is the Turkish word for 'gold', but is also a common title of the eldest son among the Turkish steppe nomads, while *Ay*, 'Moon', is a common title for both men and women.

[2] So the text of the *Povêst*, s.a. 6615 (A.D. 1107). According to the document known as the Testament of Monomakh (*Pouchenie*) the daughter of

During the reign of Svyatopolk, the foreign elements which had been gradually gaining ground in Kiev since the reign of Vladimir I continued to increase. His *voevoda* Putyata had spent three years in Byzantium, as we have seen, and belonged to a family which had been under the influence of Greek culture for at least three generations. Moreover, Svyatopolk gave offence to the citizens of Kiev by introducing the 'Jews' into the city, by whom we may perhaps understand the remnants of the Khazar stock settled in the Crimea, and still active traders. Svyatopolk continued to favour and endow the Church as his predecessors had done, and founded the Church of St Michael of the Gilded Dome. During his reign the growing discontent merely smouldered; for, as the chronicler tells us, 'Svyatopolk loved war', and would doubtless keep the military elements well occupied. But on his death in 1113 riots broke out in the city. The climax may have been accelerated by the heavy donations which, according to the Hypatian text of the *Povêst*, were made to the Church by the wife of Svyatopolk on her husband's death, for we are told that she distributed great riches among the monasteries and the priests to such an extent that everyone was amazed, 'for such things seemed impossible'.[1]

Immediately after this entry the chronicler tells us that the citizens sent an invitation to Vladimir to come and occupy the throne left vacant by his cousin's death. Vladimir delayed and the people pillaged the house of the *voevoda* Putyata, who would be the chief representative of Greek culture and influence among the laity. They also pillaged the so-called 'Jews'. The citizens again sent to Vladimir, expressing their apprehensions of the evils which would come about in the event of delay or refusal. 'Not only the house of Putyata and the officers, as well as the "Jews", will be pillaged, but the populace will fling themselves on your sister-in-law, on the *boyars*, and on the monasteries.'

Ay Epa or Apa had been taken by Vladimir as a hostage in the encounter with Bonyak on the River Sula. See the text translated by Cross in his *Russian Primary Chronicle*, p. 308.

[1] *Povêst*, s.a. 6621 (A.D. 1113).

It is quite evident that the people of Kiev were exasperated beyond endurance with the Church, the 'Greek Party', and the foreign merchants. We reflect on the amount of money which must have been spent on the Church during the preceding century, and on the fact that the Jews or foreign merchants had already got so much Russian wealth into their own hands that Vladimir Monomakh found it necessary to promulgate laws against usury. We reflect in addition on the fact that the Polovtsy were hammering at the very doors of Kiev and the other cities on the Dnêpr, plundering and pillaging the defenceless citizens and robbing the undefended churches of their newly acquired wealth, and, what was even more serious, as Monomakh pointed out in the war councils, making it unsafe for the inhabitants of the towns to go out into the fields to reap their harvests. The citizens were threatened with starvation, while the Polovtsy were planning concerted action with their allies in the north, despite the large sums of money which had been paid to them from time to time to purchase a temporary peace. The situation is quite plain. The people must either have money to purchase immunity to cultivate their lands and live; or they must have a vigorous and resolute leader who would help them to drive the enemy from their doors, and unite them into an independent people once for all. In these circumstances it is not difficult to see why they turned to Monomakh who, all his life, had consistently sought to unite the Slavonic elements of south Russia into a political and military alliance against their common foreign foe; a man to whom family and national feeling were the guiding principles in life, and who was in addition a strong and active soldier with a vigorous offensive and defensive policy.

It is not difficult to see why the *Povêst* assumed its present form at such a crisis in the ecclesiastical history of Kiev. The Church was in jeopardy, both from the native population inside the city and from the Tatar enemy who at the same moment was beleaguering the city outside, and who in the recent past had sacked and burned the monasteries of Stephen and Germanus and of the Caves. The royal donations to the Church so lavishly bestowed by the widow of Svyatopolk could only have been a source of danger rather than a safeguard at such a moment. Yet we may assume that these donations were given on such an excessive scale for a definite purpose, and in the belief that the Church could be of some material assistance in this dark hour, and in some way help to protect the vested interests of the merchants and the nobility. At a moment when money was so badly needed to buy off the enemy, its payment to the Church could only have been made as some form of investment, and with reasonable expectations of an adequate return. And these expectations were fully justified. The immediate outcome was, in all likelihood, the *Povêst*, which must have sounded like a trumpet call to rally the despairing populace of the city, and to strengthen its leaders by stressing the immediate and practical value of national and family unity in the face of the enemy. To call the *Povêst* propaganda would be unworthy of its dignity as a conscientious historical document of unique interest and importance for the history, not only of Russia, but of eastern Europe. But its more immediate and local value must have been to strengthen greatly the work of Monomakh in welding together the various Slavonic elements into a nation, in defeating the Polovtsy, and in encouraging and profiting by the culture and learning of the Church, which, as a measure of self-preservation, had lent him its intellectual support and prestige throughout one of the greatest crises of Russian history.

Now if the *Povêst* was composed about 1113, early in the principate of Vladimir Monomakh, it was officially under his auspices. It is very possible that it owed its actual inception to some member of the polished and distinguished family to which Putyata and his brother Yan belonged, and that, as I have suggested above, the ecclesiastical donations of Svyatopolk's wife were financing the scheme. Vyshata, as stated above, had spent three years in Byzantium, where he would undoubtedly acquire Greek learning, while Yan is cited by the chronicler himself as his authority for much of the information which the work contains. He is, in fact, the person most likely to have supplied the *mnoga slovesa* relating to the period before Yaroslav, and he would be specially qualified to know stories relating to Novgorod, in view of the fact that his father and his grandfather seem to have belonged there originally, while he himself functioned in the north in the heathen reaction of which the *Povêst* gives some account s.a. 6579 (A.D. 1071). He would, for example, be well qualified to recount occurrences which had taken place in Novgorod in the time of Vladimir I, where his own grandfather Ostromir must have been living as a boy at the time. Is he also responsible for the story of Vladimir's idols in Kiev, and of Dobrynya's heathen activities in Novgorod? Whatever traditions came under the notice of the chronicler, we may be sure that his first concern would be to eliminate anything which might seem to discredit Monomakh; and on the other hand he would naturally represent any action in which his prince took part in as favourable a light as possible. This partiality comes out very clearly in the prompt action which Monomakh is represented as taking consequent upon the blinding of Vasilko,[1] and more especially in the words which are put into his mouth in the councils held among the princes on this and other occasions of disunity among the descendants of Vladimir I, notably those councils in which the military activities to be undertaken against the Polovtsy are discussed.

It will be seen that Vladimir Monomakh is represented in the chronicle, both here and in the account of the rise of the populace against Putyata and Svyatopolk's widow, as the great unifying influence of western Russia, the hero of the populace, the peacemaker and constructive element in the royal family, and the rallying point for all the native and local elements against external aggression. If it were not too early to speak of nationalism in Russia we should call him a great nationalist. This is the light in which the chronicler is anxious to represent the reigning prince. We must expect the account of previous events to be coloured by this desire to represent them as leading up to a full and final fruition in the person of his hero. It is probably from

[1] *Povêst*, s.a. 6605 (A.D. 1097).

a desire to emphasise the political and 'national' significance of Monomakh, possibly even to aid him by a certain amount of propaganda, rather than from motives of religious bigotry, or active anti-Scandinavian animus, [1] that the chronicler tells us so little of the Scandinavian rule under Rurik—which would not, of course, have been of primary interest in Kiev in later times in any case; and it is with this same end in view that he minimises the importance of Oleg in the early history of Kiev.

On the other hand, these same considerations, and more especially the ecclesiastical bias of the chronicler, are equally operative when we turn to the account of the reign of Vladimir II (Monomakh) in the *Povêst*. Nevertheless, in the story of the struggle of Vladimir II against the Polovtsy we feel at once that we are in a milieu which offers ideal conditions for the development of a Cycle of heroic poetry. The prompt and resolute character of Vladimir II, and his undoubted military gifts, his single-minded devotion to his people, his personal integrity, and his sound judgment, mark him out as an ideal leader. His elder cousin Svyatopolk was, in many respects, a more brilliant figure, and more likely, with his dashing and impulsive courage, to appeal to the imagination of a heroic minstrel; but Svyatopolk lacked both the judgment and the constructive policy of his cousin. He was a better soldier than a general. Vladimir knew when to strike and how to succeed. Above all he adopted an offensive policy against the enemy who were at the point of overwhelming his people, and he did this with complete success. His success was governed and measured by his internal policy, which was to abolish all personal and family differences, and to unite the Slavonic princes, and their followers, in a common effort against the foreign invader.

Such is the picture of Vladimir II as presented to us in the *Povêst*; and, as I have already stated, it may be taken as representing fairly Vladimir's own ideals, since it must have been composed and given permanent form by his sanction. The success of his efforts must have been the standard by which his

[1] See F. Braun, *loc. cit.* p. 158.

ideals would be appraised in his own time. A prince who could broadcast a call to arms, muster and unite the various military leaders and their followers, and, under famine conditions, plan an offensive campaign against the foe at their very doors, and by dash and courage and strategy combined rout an enemy of great numerical superiority, believed to be invincible, must have been the subject of many a *slava* and heroic eulogy. We know, moreover, that the foreign elements in Kiev in his day were at least as great, if not greater, than are suggested by the foreign missions in the time of Vladimir I, and Vladimir II certainly shows himself at least not less versed in Greek learning than his ancestors. It seems probable, indeed, that the Cycle of heroic stories which recount the union of a heterogeneous assemblage of heroes under a great prince Vladimir of Kiev, and their exploits against the invading Tatars, originated in traditional reminiscences of Vladimir II and his deeds against the Polovtsy, rather than in the wars of Vladimir I against the Pechenegs.

It would be an interesting task to attempt to reconstruct the intellectual conditions prevailing in Kiev during the early years of the twelfth century. It is clear from the internal evidence of the *Povêst* that at the period of its inception the intellectual life of Kiev was extremely active, and that both oral and written literature were encouraged. In particular we can trace the history of one family for several generations, and its influence on the political destiny and the literary and traditional history incorporated in the *Povêst*. The earliest member of this family mentioned is Ostromir, who is referred to (s.a. 6572, i.e. A.D. 1064) as having been a *voevoda* of Novgorod. His son Vyshata was *voevoda* of Prince Yaroslav of Kiev, in whose service he took part in an expedition against Byzantium. His behaviour here was fully in accord with heroic tradition, and the account in the *Povêst* of his heroic self-sacrifice on behalf of his *druzhina* is reminiscent of panegyric poetry. As a result of his gallantry he was taken as a prisoner to Byzantium, where he remained for three years, no doubt acquiring something of Greek culture. The last time we hear of him is in the year 6572 (1064), when we are told that

Rostislav, the grandson of Yaroslav, fled to Tmutorakan, and Vyshata, the son of Ostromir, *voevoda* of Novgorod, fled with him.

Vyshata's sons, Yan and Putyata, were employed by Svyatopolk II in warfare against the Polovtsy. Putyata was Svyatopolk's *voevoda* in Kiev, and both he and Yan regularly acted as envoys. It is interesting to note that Putyata's house in Kiev was destroyed during the rising against the 'Jews' in 1113, in the disturbance in Kiev consequent upon the death of Svyatopolk. His brother Yan was a sage and a historian, as well as a soldier[1] and a prudent councillor.[2] He seems to have been versed in the traditional practices of Finnish shamanism, for he is credited with having encountered and disputed with two *volkhva* ('wizards') from the Volga in 1071, who were accused of destroying Russian women, and whom he afterwards slew in his missionary zeal. He and his wife Maria were both Christians.[3] The chronicler adds the interesting information that he died at the age of ninety, a pious and hearty old man, and that he was buried in the Pechersk monastery at Kiev.[4] He adds that he himself has received many of the narratives (*mnoga slovesa*) which he has inscribed in the Annals (i.e. the *Povêst*) from this Yan. All this circumstantial evidence relating to Putyata and his family, coming as it does from a contemporary chronicler, would be enough in itself to weigh heavily in the scale in favour of rejecting the account— whatever the origin of the tradition—given in the so-called Ioachim chronicle,[5] which associates Putyata and his rising with

---

[1] See the *Povêst* (ed. Miklosich), s.a. 6597 (A.D. 1089); s.a. 6614 (A.D. 1106).

[2] *Ib.* s.a. 6601 (A.D. 1093).

[3] *Ib.* s.a. 6599 (A.D. 1091).

[4] This is the famous monastery of the Caves to which belonged the monk Nestor who was formerly regarded as the author of the *Povêst*, and where the *Povêst* was, in fact, probably composed by the monk Sylvester. See Cross, *op. cit.* pp. 95 f.

[5] For a recent discussion of this version and its origin, see a valuable article by M. Gorlin, 'La Chronique de Joachim', in *Revue des Études slaves*, Vol. XIX (1939), pp. 40 ff.

the period of Vladimir I, and of accepting the account given in the *Povêst*, which associates Putyata with Svyatopolk and Vladimir II.

It will be seen that the *Povêst* has preserved for us a brief family saga covering three generations of a very intellectual family—probably the most intellectual family in Russia in their day. Ostromir, whose youth must have been passed in the lifetime of Vladimir I, is thought to have been most probably the Ostromir with whom the famous Ostromir Gospels are associated. If this is so, he must have been educated in the learning of the Greek Church. In any case his son occupied a leading position in Kiev under a ruler who earned for himself the permanent epithet of 'The Wise', and it is inconceivable that Vyshata himself did not profit fully by his three years' sojourn in the home of Greek learning. His son Putyata inherited his position of responsibility in Kiev, and by his devotion to the interests of the Church and of Greek culture, and his support of the foreign residents in Kiev, drew down upon himself in a period of economic depression the wrath of the populace, which was, it may be presumed, Slavonic. Yet the unpopularity can only have been a passing cloud; for the chronicler, whose own sympathies are strongly 'nationalistic', pays generous tribute to Putyata's brother Yan, perhaps because, despite Yan's outstanding zeal in the cause of the Greek Church, he was well versed in the native lore of his country, and was able to supply from oral tradition the sagas of old time, and perhaps poems from which the chronicler was enabled to reconstruct his picture of Varangian Kiev. At the same time the chronicler could not fail to appreciate the extent to which his Church was indebted to the support, both moral and financial, given to it by the *voevoda* Putyata.

It would have been interesting to know more about this family, which seems to have been the most highly educated and interesting family in Russia in its day, and to have governed first Novgorod, and later Kiev, under the Varangian rulers and their descendants for three generations. Nothing is told us as to their origin—Ostromir is *voevoda* of Novgorod when we first hear of him—and their position is quietly assumed throughout. Is it possible that they represent a pre-Varangian ruling element? We cannot for a moment accept the proposition that the Varangians are the originators of culture in either Kiev or Novgorod. The evidence of the traditions in the *Povêst* itself—even making due allowance for its anti-Norse bias[1]—is enough to demonstrate that Kiev had been a sanctuary and a centre of trade before the Varangians had acquired any foothold there. Whoever were ultimately responsible for this early culture, whether Khazars, or Goths, or even an earlier people, will doubtless come to light through the medium of archaeology. But it is interesting to find already flourishing at this early period an ancient enlightened family who, despite their Greek education, are soaked in Russian traditional culture and sympathies, and who can hardly have come into being as a direct result of Norse rule. The existence of such a family, as well as the important position ascribed to the Russian *voevodas* in general, make it clear that already in Slavonic Russia a vigorous cultural life was developed which was not cancelled even by the temporary Norse supremacy.

[1] On the anti-Norse bias shown in the chronicler, see F. Braun, *loc. cit.* p. 158.

APPENDIX I

Extract from IBN MISKAWAIH in *The Eclipse of the 'Abbasid Caliphate*, Vol. V (pp. 67 ff.). Translated from the Arabic by D. S. MARGOLIOUTH (Blackwell, Oxford, 1921)

Account of the exploits of the Russians and their issue

They are a mighty nation with vast frames and great courage. They know not defeat, nor does any of them turn his back till he slay or be slain. It is the practice of the individual among them to carry his armour, while bearing suspended upon his person an artisan's outfit, axe, saw, hammer, and the like. He fights with spear and shield; he wears a sword and has hung upon him a lance and an instrument resembling a poniard. They fight on foot, especially these invaders. For indeed after sailing the sea which washes their country[1] they crossed to a vast river called the Kur, which has its source in the mountains of Adharbaijan and Armenia, and flows into this sea. It is the river of Bardha'ah, which they compare to the Tigris. When they reached the Kur they were met by Marzuban's[2] officer who served as his governor of Bardha'ah at the head of three hundred Dailemites and about the same number of Su'luks and Kurds. He also summoned the people of the place to arms, and was joined by some 5000 volunteers anxious to fight these invaders. They were however under a delusion, not knowing the strength of the Russians, whom they expected to behave like Greeks or Armenians. When they met them in battle not more than an hour elapsed before the Russians made a fierce onslaught which routed the army of Bardha'ah; the volunteers and the rest of the troops turned their backs with the exception of the Dailemites, who stood their ground and were killed to a man except such of them as were

---

[1] The Caspian. [2] See above, p. 52.

mounted. The Russians then pursued the fugitives to the town, whence every one, soldier or civilian, who had a mount to carry him, fled, leaving the town to be entered and seized by the Russians.

I was informed by Abu'l-'Abbas Ibn Nudar and a number of careful enquirers how the Russians when they hurried into the town made a proclamation to the following effect to the citizens: There is no dispute between us on the matter of religion; we only desire the sovereignty; it is our duty to treat you well and yours to be loyal to us. The armies however came against them from all sides, only to be routed by the Russians, who made sorties. When the Moslems charged the Russians, the people of Bardha'ah cried out *Allah Akbar*, and flung stones at the Russians. The latter had charged the people of Bardha'ah to restrain themselves, and not interfere between them and the Sultan;[1] but though this advice was accepted by the respectable classes, the common people and the rabble would not restrain themselves, but gave vent to their feelings by attacking the Russians when the followers of the Sultan charged them. After a time they issued a proclamation that none of the original inhabitants were to remain in the town after three days from the day of the proclamation. All who had mounts to carry them, their womenfolk and their children left the place. These, however, were a small minority; when the fourth day came the majority were still there; so the Russians put them to the sword, slaughtering countless numbers. After the massacre they bound over 10,000 men and lads with their womenfolk, their wives and their daughters; they proceeded to place the women and children in a fortress within the city called locally Shahristan, where they had taken up their quarters, lodged their troops and entrenched themselves. They then gathered the men into the Public Mosque, set guards at the doors, and bade the men ransom themselves.

[1] I.e. the Moslem government (Margoliouth).

Account of a sound scheme suggested by one of them, which they declined to follow, in consequence whereof they were massacred and their goods and families were pillaged

There was in the place a Christian clerk of sound judgment, named Ibn Sam'un, who acted as negotiator between the parties, and made an arrangement with the Russians, whereby each man should be ransomed for twenty dirhems. The wiser among the Moslems acceded to this arrangement, but the others disapproved, holding that it was Ibn Sam'un's purpose to equalise the Moslems with the Christians as payers of poll-tax.[1] Ibn Sam'un therefore broke off negotiations; the Russians delayed their massacre, hoping to get this trifling amount from their intended victims. When it was not forthcoming, they put them to the sword, and indeed slew them to the last man except a few who got away in a narrow conduit which conveyed water to the Mosque, and such as purchased their lives with hoards which they happened to possess. It happened in some cases that a Moslem arranged with a Russian to buy his life for a certain sum, and went with the Russian to his house or shop. When he produced his hoard, and it turned out to be more than the sum which he had covenanted to pay, the Russian would not let him keep it, not even if it were many times more than the amount, but kept raising his demands till he had ruined the man; only when the Russian was convinced that nothing remained to him, no gold, silver, bedding or clothing, would he let him go, giving him a piece of stamped clay to serve as a safe-conduct. Thus the Russians possessed themselves of a vast amount of property. They retained the females and lads, on whom they gratified their lusts, and whom they enslaved.

[1] Probably this is corrupt for a word meaning 'ransom', since a single payment could not well be called 'poll-tax', and the Islamic law assesses at different rates the lives of different religious communities (Margoliouth).

When the terrible nature of the calamity was realised, and the Moslems in the different countries heard about it, they called for a general expedition. Marzuban b. Mohammed mustered his troops, and called for a general enlistment. Volunteers joined him from all directions. He marched at the head of 30,000 men, but in spite of the numbers that he had gathered he was unable to make head against the Russians or to produce any effect upon them. Morning and evening he used to attack them, and regularly retire defeated. The war continued to be waged in this style for many days, and the Moslems were always the vanquished.

When the Moslems found themselves unable to deal with the Russians, and Marzuban began to realise the situation, he had recourse to strategy. It so happened that when the Russians had got into Bardha'ah,[1] they indulged excessively in the fruit of which there are numerous sorts there.[2] This produced an epidemic among them, as theirs is an exceedingly cold country, where no tree grows, and the little fruit which they have is imported from distant regions. When their numbers began thereby to be reduced, Marzuban, seeking for a stratagem, bethought him of laying an ambush for them at night. He therefore arranged with his army that they should make a hurried attack; when the Russians charged, he with his followers should let themselves be routed, thereby encouraging them to hope that they would be able to annihilate the Moslem army; when the Russians got beyond the place where the ambush lay, Marzuban with his followers should return to the charge and shout to the ambush a cry on which they had agreed; when the Russians had thus got between the two forces, the Moslems would have them in their power.

The morning after this scheme had been arranged, Marzuban with his followers advanced, and the Russians came out to meet them. Their commander was mounted on an ass, and his followers came out and ranged themselves in order of battle. The usual

---

[1] The text has Maraghah, but it is not stated that they overran all Adharbaijan; this seems therefore to be a scribe's error (Margoliouth).

[2] Moses of Khorene mentions olives and cucumbers (*ibid.*).

procedure occurred. Marzuban with the Moslems took to flight, and were pursued by the Russians till they had got beyond the place of the ambush. Only the Moslems continued their flight.

Marzuban afterwards narrated how, when he saw his followers act thus, and his earnest entreaties to them to renew the fight were unavailing owing to the terror of the Russians which had seized their hearts, he recognised that if this went on, the Russians on their return would not fail to notice the ambush, which would in consequence be destroyed. So, he said, I turned round myself with my personal attendants, my brother, my staff, and my retainers, having made up my mind to die a martyr's death. Thereupon most of the Dailemites were shamed into doing the like; we charged, cried out to the ambush, which issued forth behind the Russians, fought them in brave style, and killed 700 of them, including their commander; the remainder made their way into the fortress in the town, where they had established their quarters, and whither they had moved a quantity of food and stores, and where they housed their captives and their treasures.

While Marzuban was besieging them, with no other plan than to reduce them by protracted siege, news reached him that Abu 'Abdallah Husain B. Sa'id B. Hamdan[1] had entered Adharbaijan and reached Salmas, where he had united forces with Ja'far B. Shakkuyah the Kurd, who was at the head of the Hadayan[2] hordes. Marzuban was therefore compelled to leave one of his officers to fight the Russians with 500 Dailemites, 1500 Kurdish horsemen, and 2000 volunteers; he himself proceeded to Auran,[3] where he met Abu 'Abdallah. An insignificant engagement ensued, when there was a heavy snowfall; the followers

[1] He had been Nasir al-daulah's minister of public security there previously.

[2] In Ibn Hauqal, ed. de Goeje, p. 156, the name is spelt Hadnaniyyah. These are said, *ib*. 239, to be quartered at Ushnuh near Urmiah; but the true reading should be *Hadhbānī*, and the name associated with *Adiabene* (Syrian *Hedhayab*), the ancient Assyria. I am indebted to V. Minorsky for this information.

[3] This place is not mentioned by Yaqut. Azan near Salmas on the modern maps seems likely to be meant.

of Abu 'Abdallah, most of whom were Arabs, became disorderly, and deserted him; he in consequence made for one of the fortified cities, but was met on the way by a dispatch from his cousin Nasir al-daulah, informing him of the death of Tuzun in Baghdad, and the desertion of Tuzun's troops to himself, and of his determination to descend with them to Baghdad in order to fight Mu'izz al-daulah, who had entered and taken possession of the city after Tuzun's departure upstream. He therefore ordered Abu 'Abdallah to evacuate Adharbaijan and rejoin him, which he did.

The followers of Marzuban continued to attack and besiege the Russians till the latter grew weary. The epidemic became severe in addition. When one of them died they buried with him his arms, clothes and equipment, also his wife or some other of his womenfolk, and his slave, if he happened to be attached to him; this being their practice.[1] After their power had come to an end the Moslems disturbed their graves and brought out a number of swords which are in great demand to this day for their sharpness and excellence. When their numbers were reduced, they left by night the fortress in which they had established their quarters, carrying on their backs all they could of their treasure, gems and fine raiment, and burning the rest. They dragged with them such women, boys and girls as they wanted, and made for the Kur, where the ships in which they had issued from their home were in readiness with their crews, and 300 Russians whom they had been supporting with portions of their booty. They embarked and departed, and God saved the Moslems from them.

From persons who witnessed these Russians I heard wonderful stories of their prowess and contempt of the Moslem forces gathered against them. Thus there was a story current in the region which I heard from many persons how five Russians were assembled in a garden in Bardha'ah, one of them a beardless lad of fair countenance, the son of one of their chieftains, with some captive women. When the Moslems knew of their presence,

[1] This is recorded by the other authorities on the early Russians (Margoliouth).

they surrounded the garden, and a large number of Dailemite and other troops came together to fight these five. They tried hard to get a single prisoner out of the number, but it was not possible, for none of them would capitulate, and they could not be killed before they had slain many times their number of the Moslems. The beardless lad was the last survivor. When he perceived that he was going to be captured, he mounted a tree that was near him, and kept slashing away at his vital parts with his scimitar till he fell dead.

APPENDIX II

The Scandinavian Background: *Oddr Víthförli* (*Örvar-Oddr*)

It has long been recognised that the story of Oleg, and more especially that of his death, bears a close resemblance to the story of Örvar-Oddr, the great Hálogaland hero of early Norse saga, who is known to Norse tradition as 'Oddr the Far-travelling', and who gained fame, not only among his own people, but also abroad as a result of a famous journey to Bjarmaland which he is said to have made in early life. He is also known as Örvar-Oddr because he possessed three famous arrows, known as the *Gusisnautar*, 'Gusi's treasure', which had been taken by his grandfather, Ketill Haengr, from Gusi, the king of the 'Finns'. The story of Örvar-Oddr's death is so closely similar to that of Oleg (O.N. Helgi) that there can be no possible doubt that the same story has been told of both heroes. Opinion has differed as to which is the original, but a possible solution has been found by Stender-Petersen,[1] who points out that the story is probably of Turkish origin, and that it has spread, not only to Russia and the north, but also to the Balkans, where it is found in a form closely resembling that of the Russian Oleg. It is not improbable that the story has been brought from Byzantium by Varangians, and transmitted from Varangians in Kiev to Scandinavia.[2]

The question naturally arises why the story should have become attached to Örvar-Oddr, and this, not as a single episode incorporated mechanically into his saga, but interwoven carefully into the weft of the story. The explanation would seem to lie in some feature in the original story of Oddr which has resembled the 'death story', and for which the latter has been substituted, perhaps after it had become widely known. Possibly some such

[1] *Die Varägersage als Quelle der Altrussischen Chronik* (Leipzig, 1934), pp. 176 ff.
[2] See Stender-Petersen, *op. cit.* pp. 206 ff.

explanation may underlie the introduction of the story into the account of the death of Oleg also. But there must be some close connection between the Russian and the Norse stories, independent of their common origin, because the incident of the snake is also common to both, whereas this feature seems to have been absent from the original version. It has therefore been added, in all probability in Russia. This is all the more surprising in view of the fact that in Russian oral poems known as *byliny* (sing. *bylina*), the Tatar nomad chiefs are generally represented as serpents, and the Russians are invariably represented as victorious over them. Can the story of Oleg's death from a snake bite reflect his death at the hands of the nomads? Involuntarily one thinks of the Khazar document which relates that Helgu met his death 'in Persia'. The story, in any case, seems to have been recorded in an unsympathetic milieu, by one who was not favourable to the traditions of the Norse régime in Kiev.

How then has it come to be attached to the Norse hero Örvar-Oddr in his own country? Leaving aside for the moment this local consideration, let us glance briefly at the story of Örvar-Oddr to see how far this is an isolated resemblance, and to enquire whether any other incidents in his life also resemble those of Oleg as related in the *Povêst*. Örvar-Oddr is, as I have already said, the first great hero to make the journey to Bjarmaland, and for some reason, which is not clear in the saga itself, his journey acquired special and widespread fame, and, in fact, is the chief feature associated with him in after years. Yet he belonged to a family of pioneers, and both his father, Grímr Lothinkinni, and his grandfather, Ketill Haengr, who lived at Hrafnista on or close to the island of Njarthey in the south of Hálogaland, made journeys to Bjarmaland before him. Some of the incidents related of their journeys are obviously identical with those related of Örvar-Oddr himself; but whether these are mere duplications and transferences, or whether, as would seem to be more likely, the transferences are suggested by similarity in incidents in the careers of all these heroes is a matter which we need not decide here. The important matter is that Oddr belonged to a family from Hálogaland famous for daring enterprise and difficult and distant travel among peoples virtually unknown, and that he himself is the most famous member of the family by virtue of one particular journey which he made to the famous and somewhat nebulous Bjarmaland, by which the northern territories of Novgorod are generally understood.[1]

The saga of Örvar-Oddr is a long one, and it is clear that in his person more than one hero and his exploits have been combined, and that in some cases the same story has been related twice in variant forms, as if they were quite different adventures, taking place at different periods. The hero himself is believed to have been a historical person living in the ninth century,[2] who doubtless visited Russia and the peoples of east central Europe. The saga itself is thought to be one of the oldest of the collection known as the *Fornaldar Sögur*, and the oldest manuscript belongs to the beginning of the fourteenth century. The saga can therefore not be later than the thirteenth.[3] Owing to its great length it will only be possible to refer here very briefly to a few of the episodes which relate to the milieu in which we are especially interested.

The saga opens with the birth of the hero to Lopthaena, the wife of Grímr Lothinkinni, at Berurjóthr, the home of Grímr's friend Ingjaldr, where Oddr is fostered, and where he becomes the foster-brother of Ingjaldr's son, Ásmundr. The father and son are described as great *blótmenn*,[4] and Ingjaldr invites a *völva*, or 'prophetess', called Heithr[5] to a feast early in the saga; but Oddr treats the *völva* with disrespect, scorning her supernatural powers

---

[1] For a detailed and scholarly account of the identity of Bjarmaland, see A. S. Ross, *The Terfinnas and Beormas of Ohthere* (Leeds Studies in English, 1940).

[2] See R. C. Boer, *Örvar-Odds Saga* (Halle, 1892), p. xiv.

[3] See E. Mogk, *Geschichte der Norwegisch-Isländischen Literatur* (Strassburg, 1904), p. 283.

[4] The word is generally understood to have reference to those who practised heathen sacrifice, but it more probably refers to a particular form of ancient heathen cult practice of dedication. The matter is one which urgently calls for further investigation.

[5] This is the name commonly applied to the *völur* (sing. *völva*), and is probably in reality a common noun.

and knowledge, and the *völva* retaliates by prophesying that
Oddr will be slain by his horse Faxi. In order to avert the fulfil-
ment of the curse, Faxi is killed and a barrow is raised over him,
and Oddr and Ásmundr set off to Hrafnista, Oddr's family home,
to join his father, Grímr Lothinkinni. Here he finds that Grímr's
other son Guthmundr and his nephew Sigurthr are about to sail
for Bjarmaland, and Oddr eventually decides to accompany
them, taking his foster-brother Ásmundr with him.

The fleet sails north along Finnmark, taking the course adopted
by King Alfred's informant, the Hálogalander Ohthere, till, like
him, they come to the mouth of the River Vína, which is
generally identified with the northern Dvina, where they find
many islands, and proceed to cast anchor under a great promon-
tory. Here they see a great host of men assembling out of the
woods for a feast, and Oddr and Ásmundr land to investigate,
leaving Guthmundr behind to guard the ship. It is now almost
dark, but they see a great hall (*skáli*) brightly illuminated from a
great vessel which shines inside the building with great brilliance.
There is a merry din, and the people are talking in an unknown
tongue. Oddr meanwhile descries a man who looks like a
Norseman, and who is acting as cupbearer, and they manage
to kidnap him and carry him to their ship.

The man tells them that on the banks of the Vína there is a
great barrow made of silver and earth, to which are brought
two handfuls of earth and two of silver for everyone who dies
or is born, and Oddr deputes the task of robbing this barrow to
Guthmundr and Sigurthr, while this time he himself remains
behind to guard the ship; but when they return laden with
treasure, he and Ásmundr go in their turn, and meanwhile the
cupbearer escapes and rouses the Bjarmar, and a great battle
ensues. The Bjarmar are defeated, and the Norsemen make their
escape, but a great storm arises, and it is only when they have
cast all the *finnskref* (i.e. the 'Bjarmian treasure') overboard that
the storm abates, and they are able to land.

Soon, however, they see another army assembling against
them, and after some adventures, which are very similar to

those attributed to Grímr Lothinkinni in the saga which bears his name, Oddr and Ásmundr land and find a cave occupied by trolls, who are overheard talking about Oddr himself, and plotting against his life. Oddr shoots the trolls with two of Gusi's arrows, and afterwards makes his escape back to his home in Hrafnista; and so ends Oddr's first great adventure, his journey to Bjarmaland. His journey has made him famous, and after this everywhere he goes the first question asked of him is: 'Are you the Oddr who went to Bjarmaland?' Subsequently he sails southwards to Elfarsker, and wins the warship *Hálfdanarnautr* and afterwards slays a Viking called Sóti. It would be interesting to know the relationship of this Sóti to Sóti the Viking, the brother of Thorgerthr Hölgabrúthr, to whom reference will be made again later, and whose barrow is said to have been robbed by *Hörthr* in the *Harthar Saga ok Hólmverja*, ch. 15, and also to another Sóti, who is described as a strong troll and who is said to have lived in the depths of a wood not far from the dwelling of a certain Jarl Framarr of Árhaugr in Sweden, and whose death at the hands of Oddr's grandfather, Ketill Haengr, in the course of his journey to Sweden, is described in *Ketils Saga Haengs*. It is interesting to note that the death of Sóti at the hands of Oddr also takes place as he is on his way to Sweden, so that it may be assumed that here at least the same adventure is attributed to two different generations of the same family. Oddr's winter in Sweden and his friendship with Hjálmarr at the Swedish court, which follow immediately upon the slaying of Sóti, may be presumed, therefore, to have taken the place of Ketill's sojourn at Árhaugr and his friendship with the prince Böthmóthr.

Oddr next goes raiding in the British Isles, where his friend Ásmundr is killed by a stray arrow; and here Oddr marries a 'Scottish' or, more probably, an Irish princess named Ölvör, by whom he has a daughter Ragnhildr. We are told incidentally that while in the British Isles he makes peace with a certain Skolli. It is curious to reflect that in all probability Oddr's visit would take place during the reign of King Alfred, and that if he had related his adventures to the king, they would have been

practically identical, at least in their early part, with the story
which the Hálogalander Ohthere related to King Alfred of his
own voyage to Bjarmaland and his explorations up the northern
Dvina. I confess it is extremely tempting to ask whether the
English king may not have had audience with our hero. The
name Ohthere (O.N. Óttarr) does not correspond philologically
with Oddr; but the fame of Oddr's journey might well account for its inclusion in King Alfred's translation of Orosius,
while I have always suspected that the inclusion of this voyage
in the king's geography, coming as it does immediately before
Wulfstan's pioneering work in the eastern Baltic, formed a part
of a design by King Alfred, and doubtless shared by the Norsemen
and the Danes, to open up northern Russia to the west as a through
route to the Orient. It is interesting to notice that after Oddr's
attempts to sail up the northern Dvina have failed, he gradually
makes his way to Russia by a southern route, and it would seem
that King Alfred, by placing Wulfstan's voyage to the eastern
Baltic immediately after the voyage of Ohthere, was intending to
suggest that such a route might profitably be tried (cf. p. 169 f.).

Once again Oddr and Hjálmarr sail to Elfarsker, where they
meet one of the most interesting characters in the saga, Ögmundr
Eythjófsbani, known later in the story under his real name of
Kvillanus, who, on hearing that Oddr is the man who has been
to Bjarmaland, at once offers him combat. Ögmundr, in fact,
is the great champion of the Bjarmar, who, as Oddr afterwards
learns, has been specially reared for the purpose of inflicting
vengeance on Oddr for his previous attack on the Bjarmar. He
and his men are said to be invulnerable, and more like jötnar
than men, both in size and horribleness, while he himself is
described as a hideous being with black hair and a felt hood
covering his forehead, leaving nothing visible except the teeth
and eyes.[1] But though he and Oddr fight for a long time, neither
can gain a decisive victory over the other, and eventually they

---

[1] This might well be a description of a typical occupant of the Kola
Peninsula or Russian Lapland in winter dress. But it also suggests the
costume assumed by Ragnarr Lothbrók, which was made invulnerable
and prepared for him by his wife or fosterer.

separate, and Ögmundr disappears while Oddr and Hjálmarr return to Uppsala.

A series of adventures follows, the most famous of which is the encounter of Oddr and Hjálmarr with another great family, the sons of Arngrímr, in a great battle on the island of Samsey, in which, though Hjálmarr himself is killed, Oddr is victorious, and all the sons of Arngrímr are slain. It is no doubt this great battle which settled once for all the struggle for power and prestige between these two great northern families, both of which were evidently seeking expansion and conquest. Oddr builds great barrows in which he inters the sons of Arngrímr, and then returns to Uppsala, carrying the body of Hjálmarr with him. On hearing the news of Hjálmarr's death his wife Ingibjörg dies instantly, which, taken in connection with other evidence of a similar bearing relating to the Swedish queens, suggests the probability of suttee.[1] One text, indeed, states that she took her own life.

There follow in our saga accounts of Oddr's wanderings in the land of the Franks, and in the Holy Land, till finally he is carried by a 'vulture' (*gammr*) to its nest, whence he is rescued by a certain *jötunn* called Hildir, described as a giant from Rísaland,[2] who takes Oddr to his home to be fostered by his daughter Hildigunn. Owing to Oddr's small size in comparison with the giants of Rísaland, Hildigunn places him in the cradle with her baby brother Gothmundr, but subsequently she herself has a son by him called Vignir.

Some ten years later Oddr sets off once more to look for his old enemy Ögmundr, and by chance meets his son Vignir, who tells him that Ögmundr is in Helluland, which is generally understood to be Labrador. Here they find a great stronghold and here Vignir is slain by Ögmundr, who afterwards disappears into the sea. Later Oddr learns that Ögmundr has joined himself to Geirröthr the giant and to Geirríthr his daughter; and Oddr

---

[1] See e.g. *Flateyjarbók*, I, cap. 63, and cf. further Kershaw, *Stories and Ballads of the Far Past* (Cambridge, 1921), p. 150.

[2] Is this Russia? Cf. Braun, *Festschrift für Eugen Mogk* (Halle-on-Saale, 1924), p. 192, footnote 1.

sets out once more to Russia, this time, apparently, by way of the Baltic, *í Austrveg*, to Geirröthr's dwelling (*at Geirröthargörthum*), and here he finds Ögmundr fishing. Ögmundr has by this time laid all the kings *í Austrveg* under tribute that each should send him every twelve months a warrior from among them. Oddr chases him to land, where he sings a verse, summoning Geirröthr to his aid. A great battle takes place; but Geirröthr is slain by Oddr, and Geirríthr is also slain, while Ögmundr sinks into the earth, Oddr holding on to his beard, which comes off in his hands.

Still seeking his old enemy Ögmundr, Oddr now comes, disguised in birch bark clothing, to the court of King Herrauthr of Húnaland,[1] where he meets an old man called Hárekr, who is said to be the fosterer of Silkisif, the king's daughter. Here in a contest of *skaldskap*, or 'poetry', Oddr overcomes the king's councillors, Sigurthr and Sjólfr, and on revealing his high lineage he is given a seat next the king. Subsequently he fights a great battle on behalf of Herrauthr against a certain Álfr, king of a land called Bjálkaland, and his wife Gytha or Gythja, which is, of course, simply the Old Norse word for a heathen 'priestess'. Álfr's army flees to the *borg*, and there stands the *gythja*, shooting arrows from every finger, like Thorgerthr Hölgabrúthr in the battle against the Jómsvíkings. Beside the *borg* stand *hof* and *hörgar*.[2]

It is strange that Oddr should be directed to the *borg* by Hárekr, who here figures simply as an 'old man' of Herrauthr's court; for the temple itself, with its highly militant *gythja*, at once recalls the temple with its militant *hofgythja* Kolfrosta in the *Bósa Saga*, and here also we meet with Hárekr, with King Herrauthr, and with a girl who is being fostered under Hárekr's auspices, but who is named, not Silkisif, but Hleithr. It is clear that the episode in the saga of Örvar-Oddr is a variant version

---

[1] Here and elsewhere Húnaland appears to be vaguely located somewhere in central or eastern Europe.

[2] The word *hof* is used of a heathen temple of any kind, *hörgr* (pl. *hörgar*) of some kind of shrine, perhaps of rough stone. The two words are frequently found coupled together, as here.

of that found in the *Bósa Saga*, though in the latter Herrauthr is represented as a king, not of Húnaland, but of Gautland. The discrepancy is probably to be accounted for by the common confusion of Gautland with Gotaland, 'the land of the Goths', or Reithgotaland, which is associated in the *Fornaldar Sögur* with Húnaland, 'the land of the Huns'. In the saga of Örvar-Oddr, Oddr overcomes Álfr and the *gythja*, and marries Silkisif the daughter of King Herrauthr.

The conclusion of the saga is very striking, and would no doubt throw valuable light on the history of the early settlement of the Norsemen in Russia if we were able to interpret the record. We are told that the king of Hólmgarthr died suddenly, and that an unknown man calling himself Kvillanus had succeeded to the kingdom. He wears a mask, and no one has seen his face, or knows his native district or his lineage, or whence he has come. Oddr sets out to Russia, and comes to Hólmgarthr. We are now told that there are many kings in *Gartharíki* (Russia), all tributary to King Kvillanus, and that these include Marró (Murom), Ráthstafr (Rostov), Eddval (Suzdal), Hólmgeirr (Novgorod), and many others from Carelia, etc. Svartr, the son of Geirríthr, is also there. Kvillanus has collected his army three years previously, and it is thought that he is anticipating Oddr's arrival. But in the encounter which follows the two sides prove themselves evenly matched, and are about to make peace, when Kvillanus raises his mask, and Oddr discovers that he is his old enemy Ögmundr, and challenges him once more to battle on the following day. In this encounter Oddr kills all the tributary kings and also Svartr; but again we are told that an arrow flies from every finger of Kvillanus, and a man dies from each arrow, and so all Oddr's men are slain. When night falls, Kvillanus draws off his sixty survivors, all wounded, into his citadel, and rules Hólmgarthr long afterwards. Oddr, however, goes away *á merkr ok skóga* till he comes to Gallia where two kings rule called Hjörólfr and Hróarr. Oddr kills Hróarr, and helps the young Hjörólfr to regain the kingdom which Hróarr had usurped at the slaying of Hjörólfr's father.

Oddr now returns to his kingdom secretly. Some time later, however, Kvillanus sends rich presents to Oddr, both gold and silver, and many costly treasures, and therewith his friendship and treaty. Oddr accepts these treasures, for he realises that Ögmundr Eythjófsbani, who is also called Kvillanus, is invincible, for he is more like a spirit than a man. 'And it is not reported that they have any more relations after this.'

The concluding chapter of the saga is, however, very interesting. Oddr and Silkisif, we are told, have two sons, Ásmundr and Herrauthr. Oddr decides to go and see to his patrimony in Hrafnista. On his return journey he goes to look where his horse Faxi is buried, and, while he is at Faxi's grave mound, an adder springs out from under the skull and bites him so that he dies, thus fulfilling the prophecy of the *völva* Heithr (see p. 147 above). Before he dies, however, he makes a long poem while his stone coffin is being prepared, and wood is being brought for the burning. He then orders that the poem be taken to Silkisif and his sons, after which he dies and is burnt. Silkisif and Hárekr rule the kingdom until Oddr's sons grow up. 'Then the line sprung from Oddr in Russia (Gartharíki) grew up. And the daughter born to Oddr in Ireland called Ragnhildr made her way to Hrafnista, and there married, and another of Oddr's lines flourished there.'

Two points to be specially noted in the concluding portions of the saga are the close connection of the fate of Oddr himself with that of his horse Faxi, and the persistent tradition that he met his death from a snake bite. The former is undoubtedly to be associated in some measure, however indirectly, with a special cult of the horse which is a feature of the religious beliefs and practices of the early Swedes and Hálogalanders. We find it in the story of the horse sent to King Gothgestr of Ömth in the Lofoten Islands by King Athils of Sweden, by means of which King Gothgestr met his death, just as Athils also met his death by a fall from his own horse 'in the temple of the *dís*', whatever the precise meaning of this obscure phrase. We also find in the *Ynglingasaga* a number of the early kings of Sweden who are similarly stated to have met their deaths in some obscure manner connected with their horses. The *völva*, in prophesying the death of Oddr from his horse, however hostile her intentions in her prognostications, would seem to be prophesying no more than that he should meet his death in the manner of the early Swedish kings, and their converts or allies in Hálogaland.[1]

Traces of this same cult of the horse are to be found also in the *Flateyjarbók*, where the milieu from which the stories are drawn would seem on the whole to be less aristocratic than that of the *Heimskringla*. We find traces of this in a curious story which relates to the phallic cult of a horse represented by a fetich called *Völsi*,[2] which may also lie behind the story of the original founder of the Völsung family. We see it again in the story of the death of Thorgerthr Hölgabrúthr in the *Flateyjarbók* and in an obscene joke at Thorgerthr's expense in the same text (*Flateyjarbók*). Such a cult is possibly connected with the curse worked by Egill Skallagrímsson by means of a horse's head stuck on a pole. It is possible that the whole horse cult is connected with the Slavonic deity Volos, who is commonly thought to be the only Russian deity of whom we have reliable evidence. It is important to bear these facts in mind here because they make it extremely probable that the close association of Oddr with his horse is an original feature of his story, though the actual form in which the story has reached us has been modified by external influence, as we have seen.

The tradition which associates the death of Oddr with a snake bite is equally significant. It is a common motif of the stories of heroes who go to Bjarmaland, and encounter King Hárekr, that they end their days by the bite of a snake or dragon. And such a fate is especially associated with the descendants of Sigurthr Hringr and notably with his son Ragnarr Lothbrók, who is said

[1] All through the early sagas it is clear that the true affinities and close relations of Hálogaland lie, not with Norway to the south, but with Sweden to the east, with which overland communications were much easier.

[2] *Flateyjarbók* II, cap. 265. The word is perhaps connected with the Greek word φαλλός.

to have met his death in an *ormgarthr*, which is almost certainly a stone burial chamber. According to the genealogies contained in the saga of Örvar-Oddr and the *Bósa Saga*, Ragnarr would be the son-in-law of Herrauthr, the father of Oddr's wife Silkisif, for according to Ragnarr's own saga and that of his sons he himself is the husband of Herrauthr's daughter Thóra. In any case Oddr's connection with his family would seem to be close. In other stories Hárekr himself has the power to turn himself into a flying dragon, and in the *Thorskfirthinga Saga* his son Valr and his grandsons are also flying dragons. The story of Oddr's death from the snake bite, therefore, has probably been attached to the hero, like the story of the horse, in view of some similar story which had been previously associated with him.

It will be seen that the career of the early Russian ruler Oleg, as we find it in the pages of the *Povêst*, has much in common with that of the Norse saga hero Örvar-Oddr, in addition to the virtually identical accounts of their death. Like Oddr, Oleg comes by stealth to a great and wealthy stronghold somewhere in Russia in which there are men who understand the Norse tongue. Like Oddr he leaves his men in the boats, and in ambush in the woods, and raids and robs the stronghold. Like Oddr's his early adventures are in the north of Russia, in the great Novgorod domains, his later ones farther south; and like Oddr's his longest and greatest journey is said to be to the East. Whereas Oddr goes to the Holy Land and is baptised in the Jordan, however, Oleg goes to Byzantium in hostile spirit. There is, however, a hint that Oleg himself may have renounced heathenism in the story of his contempt for magicians, which brought about the evil prophecy of his death, while he is said to have married his ward Igor to Olga,[1] who afterwards became a Christian. Even before this, in the words of the chronicler, 'many of the Varangians were Christians', and a church of St Elias is said to have been already in existence.[2]

[1] The chronology of Igor's early life is difficult to accept. See Laehr, *Die Anfänge des russischen Reiches* (Berlin, 1930), p. 129.

[2] *Povêst*, s.a. 6453 (A.D. 945).

It is tempting to ask whether it is possible that in the account of Oddr's eastern journeys—his early visit to Bjarmaland, which was evidently famous far and wide; his later visit to Russia proper; and his visit to the Holy Land—we have reminiscences of the conquests of Oleg, not from a wholly Slavonic population, as is so often supposed, but, as we are now coming to realise, from earlier Norse settlers. We have seen that Oleg, on approaching Kiev, found it in the possession of two *boyars* (the word is probably here used as a translation of O.N. *jarlar* or *hersar*), who were quite possibly from Hálogaland.[1] Similarly in the saga of Örvar-Oddr it is clearly implied that Russia was already in some measure occupied by Norse-speaking people, and people who understood the Norse tongue, as the story of the Norse cup-bearer in Bjarmaland early in the saga makes clear. It is interesting to notice that this man's sympathies are represented as being, not with the Norse raiders, that is to say, with Oddr and his party, but with the earlier occupants of the land; for we are told that at the earliest opportunity he makes his escape and informs the Bjarmar of Oddr's whereabouts. The struggle was certainly in a large measure one of Norsemen against Norsemen.

We have already seen that an appreciable number of the names appended to the so-called treaty of Oleg with Byzantium in the Russian *Povêst* are also to be found in close association with Oddr in the saga which bears his name. And though, as I have said, it would be a mistake to lay too much stress on these names, which are not rare elsewhere, their occurrence here is interesting. On the other hand the difference in the names of the two heroes Oleg and Oddr need be no obstacle to the possible identification of the two heroes. A careful perusal of the sagas, and more especially the collection known as the *Fornaldar Sögur* and the poems of the *Elder Edda*, leaves the impression that the name Helgi (Rus. Oleg) is not a name but a title, and originally referred

[1] The testimony of the sagas leaves no room for doubt that in the early part of the Viking Age Hálogaland was a great centre of maritime activity and enterprise.

to some kind of religious function or qualification, the nature of which has not been clearly apprehended. It seems clear, however, that it is in some way connected with the barrow, and with the cult of the dead interred in the barrow. And here it must be mentioned that Snorri tells us[1] of a certain King Helgi, who is said to have been the eponymous founder of Hálogaland,[2] and to have built a great barrow of alternate layers, one of earth and stones and one of silver or gold, exactly like the one which Oddr robs on the northern Dvina, and that in this were buried both Helgi himself and his daughter, Thorgerthr Hölgabrúthr, or, as the name is also written, by a very natural variation, Hörgabrúthr. It may be added that according to the Danish historian, Saxo Grammaticus, Thorgerthr, whom Saxo calls Thora, is said to be Helgi's wife,[3] and she is here represented as the daughter of Cusi, 'king of the Finns and Bjarmar', the enemy of Oddr's grandfather, Ketill Haengr, and the original owner of the arrows from which Oddr takes his nickname.

Oddr's name means 'Arrow-Point', and is in all probability a nickname, like so many other names of the Viking Age. It is not necessarily the one under which he was best known even in his own day, or the one under which he appears on the genealogies. In all probability both Helgi and Oddr are known elsewhere in tradition under other names. Oddr, like Helgi, was a great barrow builder. We have seen him building a great barrow for his horse Faxi; and also a group of barrows for the sons of Arngrímr after the great battle on the island of Samsey. Moreover he himself is interred in an elaborate barrow after his death—apparently the same one as that in which his horse has been buried earlier, or else another close by. If we could suppose these two great Hálogaland barrow builders, both of whom are probably

[1] In the *Prose Edda* (*Skaldskaparmál*, ch. 44).

[2] From other sources we learn that the founder of the royal line of Hálogaland was one Saemingr, who appears on some lists as one of the sons of Arngrímr, though in the *Hrómundar Saga Greipssonar*, ch. 4, he is said to have been a king in Sweden. The two statements are not necessarily incompatible.

[3] Book III, cap. 72; Elton's translation (London, 1894), pp. 87 f.

known elsewhere under a different name, to have been originally identical, it would be easier to see why both are so closely connected with Cusi or Gusi, the father of Helgi's bride. This question, however, raises the difficult problem of the exact relationship of Oddr's horse Faxi to Thorgerthr. The name Faxi means 'having a (fine) mane', and it is also said to have been the name of a stallion sacred to the god Freyr in Iceland, whom no one was allowed to mount. (See *Hrafnkels Saga Freysgotha* ch. 3 f.)

Leaving aside these difficult questions for the moment, let us turn again to consider the story of Oleg and his first appearance in the pages of the *Povêst*. It is a curious fact that we are never told anything of his home or family. It is perhaps still more surprising that we never hear of his marriage. He seems to have had the right to marry Olga to his ward; but we are not told why or how he comes to possess the right. Her name certainly represents Helga, the feminine of Helgi, and of Oleg, and it suggests that she was his daughter. Is it possible that, like Thorgerthr to Helgi, she is in some ritual sense his wife also? If this were possible, the entire picture of the relations of Oleg, Olga and Igor would at once become clear, for it would seem to be a typical piece of the form of supernatural fosterage of which the *Fornaldar Sögur* offer us a number of examples. According to this supposition, Olga would have been Igor's foster mother and foster sister before she became his wife. Such a suggestion removes the story of the relationship from the realm of history to that of oral tradition and saga; but there can be hardly any doubt that the part of the *Povêst* which here comes in for consideration is based on oral saga, and that it has its roots in a type of Scandinavian saga which is not likely to be an isolated example in Russia, but to follow a conventional Norse pattern, part of which may well originate in traditional motifs based ultimately on heathen religious cults long forgotten, and probably misrepresented, yet still containing formulae derived from the original ritual and the subsequent Norse literary tradition.

If we could accept the suggestion that Oleg came in all probability originally from Hálogaland, this would help to account for Russian ignorance as to his home and family, as also in the case of Askold and Dir. If it were possible to identify Oleg with Örvar-Oddr, it would be in no way surprising that no wife is clearly attributed to Oleg in the *Povêst*, since Oddr himself is said to have married only two wives, one from the British Isles and one from Húnaland. No Scandinavian wife is attributed to him. Moreover such an identification would in no way preclude Oleg's having come to Russia more immediately from Sweden, since we know that Oddr was a great friend and ally of Hjálmarr, the Swedish prince, and spent at least two winters at the Swedish court.

It will be seen that the suggestion which I have made involves two different equations. The first is the suggestion that the Russian Oleg is identical with the Norse Örvar-Oddr. The second is that Örvar-Oddr was also known to Scandinavian tradition under the name Helgi (Russ. Oleg), and that he is the Helgi to whom Snorri ascribes the origin of the ruling house of Hálogaland. Let us look at the second suggestion first, to see if the story of Oddr as we find it in the saga offers any justification for such an identification, apart from his importance in the ruling line, and his fame as a barrow builder. How do the stories of Oddr's marriages compare with the story of Thorgerthr, who is said by Snorri to be a daughter of Helgi, but whose name implies that she was his bride, as she is also in Saxo's narrative?

We have seen that Oddr first marries a princess from the British Isles, who bears him a daughter Ragnhildr, who subsequently makes her way to Oddr's home at Hrafnista, and of whom we hear little save that one line of Oddr's descendants trace their ancestry to her. His second wife is Silkisif, the daughter of King Herrauthr from Húnaland, who is said to have been fostered by an old man called Hárekr. It has already been pointed out that this story is only a slight variant of that contained in the *Bósa Saga*. The story itself in its general outline is the same, and most of the proper names are also identical. In the story of Oddr, however, Herrauthr is the father of the bride, not, as in the *Bósa Saga*, the wooer, while the place of the wooer is filled in our saga by Oddr himself. Moreover, while in the *Bósa Saga* the heroine's name is Hleithr, in our saga it is Silkisif. In the *Bósa Saga* the maiden is fostered by King Hárekr's mother, Kolfrosta; in our saga she is fostered by Hárekr himself, while her father's enemy is a female being who corresponds in her general features to Kolfrosta. Without attempting to decide which are the original features in these small matters of detail, which would involve us in further variants in other sagas, and would not assist our present purpose, let us look more closely for a moment at the figure of Silkisif, Oddr's own wife in the present saga.

Her name is unusual, and is generally compared with that of Ellisif, the wife of Yaroslav the Wise, the son of King Vladimir I of Kiev. The name Ellisif is generally thought to be a Russian form of Elizabeth; but this is surely hardly likely. The name Elizabeth is not common at an early date, and the second element looks like that in the name of Oddr's wife Silkisif. It seems to me probable that Ellisif and Silkisif belong to the same milieu, and that this is the country to the south-west of Russia, more especially that commonly referred to in the sagas as Húna-land, which probably includes the territory known in the *Povêst* as Dereva, and which seems to have been the personal estate of Prince Igor, where he is said to have been murdered and buried.

Now there is considerable evidence for the name Sif in Norse records, where it is associated more particularly with eastern Europe. 'Sif or Síbil' [1] is the name of Thor's wife, who is mentioned by Snorri in the Prologue to the *Gylfaginning* as being renowned for her hair, and as being the most beautiful of women, though Snorri adds that her origin is unknown, and he tells us immediately afterwards that Thor at that time was absent in the eastern Baltic, as if the two considerations were in some way connected with one another. Elsewhere he tells us that Loki cut off all Sif's hair, and that Thor forced him to supply her with golden hair, forged by the dwarves in its place. Evidently the

---

[1] Probably to be identified with the second element in the name *Mer-* or *Mar-síbil*, *Massíbil*, found elsewhere in the sagas.

only clear tradition about Thor's wife in Norse mythological tradition was that of her remarkable hair.

Now according to the tradition preserved in the *Bósa Saga*, the name of Herrauthr's mother was Sylgja, who had been married to Hringr, the king of East Gautland. The name of his daughter is there given, not as Silkisif, but as Thóra. It seems to me that the name Silkisif may well be a form of Sylgja combined with that of Sif, though the names *Sylgja* and *Silki* are not exact philological equivalents. That the element -*Sif* is the same as that of Thor's wife, however, there can, I think, be little doubt. It is by no means rare in the part of the world where Oddr is said to have met Silkisif, and occurs in the name *Sif-ka*, variously given to the Bjarmian and the Hunnish wives of King Heithrekr in the *Hervarar Saga*. It is doubtless connected also with that of *Sifeca* in the Anglo-Saxon poem *Widsith*, where it is associated, as in the *Hervarar Saga*, with Arngrímr's descendants, Hlithe (O.N. Hlöthr) and Incgentheow (O.N. Angantýr). Perhaps the Sibich of the *Thithreks Saga*, although Sibich is represented as a man, is the same name. Be that as it may, I myself associate all the *Sif* names to which I have drawn attention with the 'Siwa, dea Polaborum', 'Sifa or Sif, the goddess of the Polabi', a Slavonic people living to the west of the lower Elbe, referred to by Helmhold in a list of the deities of the Slavs known in his day.[1]

It is very probable that Helmhold's Siwa is identical with Thor's wife, and it is because she is located primarily on the Continent that Snorri is vague as to her origin. The stress laid on her hair by Snorri is important in view of the marriage of Oddr to Silkisif, for in the variant version of this story found in the *Bósa Saga*, the heroine Hleithr, who is being 'fostered' by Hárekr's mother, is found by the hero tied to her chair in the *hof* or temple by her hair. Evidently, therefore, the hair still retained its traditional importance, even in this fuller and more romantic version of the story. Nothing is said in our story of Silkisif's hair; but it is just worth noting that the name of Oddr's

[1] *Cronica Slavorum* (*Script. Rer. Germ.*, Leipzig, 1909), cap. LII.

horse, whose life is so closely bound up with his own, and who was buried in an elaborate barrow with him, is also Faxi, 'Mane'

In the *Bósa Saga* the name given to the daughter of Herrauthr and Hleithr is not Silkisif, but Thóra, the name under which Thorgerthr Hölgabrúthr is known to Saxo. Our earliest sources of knowledge for Thorgerthr Hölgabrúthr are poems on the Battle of the Jómsvíkings by various skalds, and here Thorgerthr is referred to as Gerthr and Hölgabrúthr, and represented as standing on the prow of the ship of Jarl Hákon of Hlathir, and shooting arrows from the tips of every finger, exactly as the *Gythja* in Oddr's saga. Now Thóra, the daughter of Herrauthr, is represented in more than one Norse saga as possessed of a famous snake which had been hatched out of an egg from a temple in Bjarmaland, whence it had been brought by her mother Hleithr to Gautland on her rescue from the mother of King Hárekr in the temple in Bjarmaland. It is clear from the context that this is a sacred snake such as we find evidence for at a later date in the sanctuaries of the Lithuanians and Old Prussians. It is possible that Thóra's bower, which her snake encircled and which appears to be a stone structure outside the royal dwelling, is neither more nor less than a stone barrow. I take it that this Thóra, daughter of King Herrauthr in the *Bósa Saga*, corresponds to Silkisif in the Örvar-Oddr's saga, and that her name is merely a descriptive name showing her connection with the god Thor, like that of Thorgerthr herself. But the name Thóra is also an alternative to that of Thorgerthr Hölgabrúthr, whom we have also seen to be closely associated with a famous barrow. Helgi is simply the title of the man who marries her and occupies the barrow with her, as Ragnarr Lothbrók marries Thóra. Ragnarr, however, is ultimately himself killed by snakes, in an *ormgarthr* or barrow, according to Norse tradition. Perhaps Oddr's death from a snake bite, as related in the well-known story attached also to Oleg, has been substituted for an original death from the snake connected with the cult introduced by his wife Silkisif (or Thóra), like that of Ragnarr Lothbrók himself. We may remember that according to the genealogy contained in the *Bósa Saga*, Ragnarr's wife is herself a granddaughter of Sylgja, the wife of King Hringr of East Gautland.

The name Thorgerthr, which connects Hölgabrúthr so closely with Thor, and the alternative name Thóra are possibly therefore alternatives of Sif, the wife of Thor, and of Silkisif, the wife of Oddr. Perhaps this is why Oddr is described in his saga as killing King Herrauthr's enemy Geirröthr by shooting him through the chest, as Thor pierces Geirröthr the giant, while Oddr finally dispatches Gythja by the same means as those by which Thor slays Geirríthr, the daughter of Geirröthr. Oddr is in some ritual way here thought of as the representative of the god Thor.

Now we have a large literature in Norse which relates the journeys of mortals to the realm of Geirröthr, or of his neighbour King Hárekr, and the journey is taken through the realms of a certain Guthmundr of Glasisvellir. In a number of these stories the hero who undertakes this journey is called either Helgi, or some name compounded with Thor, or by both names. Helgi seems to be a special title of those who have made the journey. The journey itself seems to be something in the nature of a religious mystery, but in the many stories in which it has been preserved, it is related simply as a geographical journey, and Helgi as the traveller who undertakes it. In the *Bósa Saga* Herrauthr himself undertakes the journey through the realm of Guthmundr of Glasisvellir to that of Hárekr. It seems to me that in the variant before us the same journey is made by Oddr, who first comes to the court of Herrauthr, and encounters Hárekr, and eventually wins Sif after slaying Geirröthr. The association of Sif with Guthmundr of Glasisvellir is preserved in the name Sif-ka, which in the *Hervarar Saga* (ch. 8) is borne by the daughter of the king of Húnaland, whose name is there not Herrauthr, but Humli, while Sifka herself marries Heithrekr, the grandson of Guthmundr of Glasisvellir.

It would seem probable, therefore, that Oddr's wife Silkisif has acquired her name from the cult with which she is connected in

her home in eastern Europe, and that according to traditions preserved in various sagas, this cult was known also in Scandinavia,
both in Gautland and in Hálogaland, to both of which areas
it was introduced, according to tradition, by the marriage of a
hero into the royal line of Bjarmaland or a neighbouring country.
This cult was probably that of Thorgerthr Hölgabrúthr. It is
closely connected with a barrow which is also a snake sanctuary,
and a number of Norse stories would seem to suggest that the
hero himself inevitably meets his end in a snake sanctuary,
apparently the same as that in which he had first associated himself with the cult by killing the snake and marrying the girl with
long hair who is its victim.

Is it possible that in the story of Oddr's death from the bite
of the snake which comes out of the skull of his horse Faxi,
'Hair', or 'Mane', itself buried in a magnificent barrow, we have
a substitution of the horse for the hero's wife, Hölgabrúthr?
If so may we suppose that in the original version, Oddr was
killed by the snake from the tomb, not of his horse, but of his
wife, and that, like Helgi, the King of Hálogaland, he was himself buried with her in the same barrow? I suspect that here the
name Faxi originates in the hair of Sif, Thor's wife, and that the
picturesque detail which represents the bride as tied into her
seat as she sits alive in her *hof* is an original feature, the horse
being a later rationalisation, originating in the cult of the horse
which prevailed in Sweden and Hálogaland, and with which
Thorgerthr is intimately associated (cf. p. 155 above). Some
relic of this original association may be preserved in the name
Mar-síbil[1] (see p. 161 above).

Before leaving the subject of Faxi, one other point comes in
for consideration. We have seen that the great foes of Oddr in
early life are the sons of Arngrímr, the two youngest of whom are
known as the two Haddingjar. Saxo knows Hadingus as one of the
early kings of Denmark, and the relations of Haddingr and Helgi
Haddingjaskati may have formed the subject of a lost *Haddingja
Saga* and of the lost poem known to tradition by the title of the

[1] The word *marr* is an O.N. poetical word for a 'steed'.

Káruljóth, from the name of Helgi's lover Kára. Now no one who has read Saxo's account of King Hadingus can fail to be struck by his similarity to the god Njörthr. Without spending time on drawing a comparison here, I will merely point out that the O.N. name Haddingr seems to be derived from the *haddr*, 'the coiffure'. It is curious that Njörthr, whom he resembles so closely, is especially associated with Hálogaland, having married Skathi, who 'goes on skis', and resembles the mountain Lapps.

Now Oddr's family, living on Njarthey ('Njörthr's Island'), must have been devotees of Njörthr.[1] Ketill Haengr is said to have grown extremely angry at once if the name of Óthinn was mentioned in his presence. But Njörthr is known to have been originally a female deity, Skathi, a male. Njörthr, moreover, is probably originally identical with the goddess Nerthus, whose shrine was on an island in the Baltic. If she is originally connected with Haddingr it is tempting to associate her with Sif, the wife of Thor whose hair was so famous, and who is said also to have been the goddess of the Polabi. Oddr's marriage to one owing loyalty to such a cult would be readily understandable in view of the loyalty of his own family to Njörthr, while the probability that his own horse Faxi, 'Mane', has been substituted in the story for his wife becomes still more strong if his wife is closely connected with the cult of Njörthr, originally a female deity, and apparently connected in some way with *haddr* and Haddingr. If this is possible, it helps to account for the extremely rich barrow constructed by the early Hálogaland King Helgi, whose wealth may be connected with his function as Haddingjaskati.

It must be confessed that my suggested identification of the Russian Oleg (Helgi) with the Norse Helgi, of Hálogaland, and the hero Örvar-Oddr, also of Hálogaland, is at best a tissue of uncertain possibilities, and more or less probable conjectures. But we may pause at this point and ask whether, in the nature of the case, the suggestion is not inherently probable. At the

---

[1] According to *Vafthrúthnismál*, Njörthr's temples and shrines are numbered by hundreds.

time with which we are dealing, Hálogaland was in process of colonisation, or great political changes, which seem to have been brought about in the main by the instrumentality of the Swedish kings. We have seen traditions which represent the family of Oddr during three generations forming alliances of friendship with the Swedish rulers. We have seen the deadly enmity of this family with its seat at Hrafnista against the family of Arngrímr's sons, who doubtless stood in the way of their rising power. Saxo[1] knows Arngrímr as a champion from Sweden, who had conquered both the Bjarmar and the Lapps of Finnmark at the instigation of Erik, the Swedish king, and forced them to pay a tribute of skins. But according to the early chapters of the *Hervarar Saga*, he dwelt on the island of Bólm off Hálogaland, and it is from Bólm that he and his sons sail south to the island of Samsey where the great battle takes place between themselves and Örvar-Oddr.[2]

The family of Örvar-Oddr would seem to be indigenous in Hálogaland. Their genealogy is derived from intermarriage between *troll* stock and the people of the land; and their home at Hrafnista, their connection with Njörthr and hostility to Óthinn, and their intercourse with the Lappish king—*Gusi Finna konungr*—mark them as the ancient rulers of at least an important part of southern Hálogaland. On the other hand the sons of Arngrímr may well have been recent arrivals in their island home of Bólm, where they had possibly established themselves by their conquest of the Bjarmar and of the Lappish king. In his hostility to Arngrímr's sons Oddr was possibly fighting to defend the ancient territorial rights of his own family and of their allies, and it is interesting to find that both he and his grandfather Ketill Haengr are traditionally represented as extremely anxious to enlist the friendship of the Swedes, with whom the native Hálogaland dynasty had always had close relations, and on whom they had probably always been in some measure dependent (cf. p. 155

---

[1] Book v; Elton's translation, p. 203.
[2] Saxo, *loc. cit.*; *Hervarar Saga*, ch. 3. See however Birger Nerman, *Studier över Svärges Hedna Litteratur* (Uppsala, 1913), pp. 140, 158.

above). Whatever the origin of the great feud between the line of Ketill at Hrafnista and that of his enemies, Arngrímr's sons, the matter was settled once for all by the great battle at the sanctuary of Óthinn on Samsey, and the memory of the battle and of Oddr's decisive victory was widely celebrated in song and saga, and has even found its way into the pages of the Danish writer Saxo.

According to Saxo, the previous exploits of Arngrímr had been undertaken in order to qualify the hero by brave deeds to be a son-in-law of Frótho, king of Denmark; and Saxo goes on to tell us, immediately after his account of the battle of Samsey, that Frótho sailed to attack Great Britain and Ireland. Now we have seen that according to the saga of Örvar-Oddr, Oddr also goes raiding in the British Isles, both in Great Britain and in Ireland. It is not easy to say whether Oddr's attack on our islands is connected with that of Frótho, in view of Saxo's confused chronology. Oddr's attack takes place, according to the saga, before the battle of Samsey, whereas Frótho's would seem to be subsequent to the battle. But it is interesting to find both attacks placed in some kind of relationship to the battle, especially in view of the fact that Frótho's brings him into contact with Kervillus, leader of the Irish, while Oddr is also said to have married an Irish princess. Is Oddr at this time in some kind of alliance with the Danes as a result of his victory over the sons of Arngrímr? And if so, what is the bearing of the alliance which he is said to have made with a certain Skolli in England? A comparison of the various texts of Oddr's saga leaves on one the impression that Oddr's attack on England is inspired by a desire to make reprisals for Skolli's attack on the Scandinavian kingdom in Northumbria; but when Skolli explains that his attack on Northumbria was in its turn inspired by a desire for vengeance because the king had slain his own father and deprived him of the kingdom which was his by right, Oddr ceases hostilities, and swears an oath before twelve men, here called *boendr*, 'land-owners', but undoubtedly the *lögmenn*, the 'Lawmen' who form one of the most important institutions of Scandinavian administration in the times to which the sagas relate, and also of the Danelaw of England. By this oath he swears fealty to Skolli, and enters his *lith*, which doubtless means his *hirth*, and then they harry and slay the king of Northumbria, and the foster-brothers, Oddr and Hjálmarr, rule Northumbria, and subsequently take the title of *Jarlar*, 'Earls'.

Who Skolli is we do not know. Eventually, we are told, the foster-brothers hand over their territory to Skolli on their departure. It is not clear from the text whether the territory in question is in the north or the south of the country. One text has it that the battle was fought in the south, and against a king Játmundr (Edmund), while the other text says nothing of the south, or of Játmundr, merely specifying a king of Northumbria. Skolli is referred to in both texts as a Viking, and as having a number of ships, forty according to one text, sixty according to the other; but the battle is stated to have been fought on land. Unfortunately the saga hardly offers us sufficient data to enable us to identify the battle.

Turning, however, to Anglo-Saxon records (cf. p. 149 above), in King Alfred's translation of the History of the World by Orosius, a considerable amount of material derived from contemporary information has been inserted into the text (cf. p. 150 above). In particular, near the beginning of the work, a long passage is inserted which describes the account given to 'his lord King Alfred' by a Hálogalander called Ohthere (O.N. Óttarr) of a voyage which he has made from his home in Hálogaland, round the North Cape perhaps to the northern Dvina; of how he had sailed up the river for some distance, and found the land in good order and populous, but inhabited by a people so hostile that he had been unable to land, and of how he had been forced to turn back. The people were called Beormas (O.N. Bjarmar). Ohthere tells the king that the people have related many narratives (*fela spella*) to him, but that he does not know how far they are to be relied on. He states that he made the voyage for purposes of exploration, and he tells the king that he was a whale fisher. The narrative opens without any further introduction than the words:

'Ohthere told his lord King Alfred that his home was the farthest north of any of the Norwegians, but on the west coast.'

Many questions at once arise in the mind of the reader of this most interesting narrative. First of all, why does the writer call King Alfred Ohthere's 'lord'? What was the exact relationship in which they stood to one another? It is surely strange that just at the moment when the king was engaged in a life and death struggle against Ohthere's compatriots, the trader should be peaceably visiting him, and recognising him as his 'lord'.

Incidentally it should be pointed out that King Alfred can hardly, as has been generally supposed, have himself made the insertion into his translation. The opening words make it clear that the narrative is the insertion of some other hand than the king's. The same redactor is probably also responsible for some or all of the remaining insertions. Of these the most interesting is an account, which follows immediately upon the insertion just referred to, of another voyage, this time of a certain Wulfstan, who is said to have set out from Hedeby (Sleswick), and to have sailed eastwards along the southern shores of the Baltic, and who has left on record some extremely interesting ethnological details of the various peoples with whom his voyage brought him into contact. His voyage is only described as far as the country occupied by the Aestii, a people at that time living in East Prussia, and nothing is said of the man himself, or of his home or occupation; nothing of how his narrative comes to be recorded, or of whether he also visited King Alfred. It is, however, significant that his narrative takes up the thread just where Ohthere's had dropped it. Both were evidently aiming at the same goal, the great waterways of Russia. Ohthere was a trader, and though no reason for the particular voyages in question is given, it is clear that the men are pioneers seeking contact at least with Russia, and perhaps with the East by some route hitherto little known in the West.

In view of these facts it is surely not without significance that immediately before the insertion of these voyages, we have, also inserted in the text of Orosius, a lengthy account of the ethnography of eastern and northern and central Europe—the earliest since Ptolemy. For this also there is no warrant in the original text of Orosius. Some hand, presumably not that of the king himself, has thought fit to bring the document up to date as a compendium of the geography of Europe, but with a distinct bias towards a special interest in Russia, and its possible approaches, whether those already known to some extent, overland through Europe, or those as yet unexplored, or little known to our people, by way of the northern Dvina, or by way of the Baltic.

The question naturally arises: How did the interpolator get his information? The narrative of Ohthere's voyage is simply the summary of a saga, such as, if expanded, would seem to offer comparison with the voyage of Örvar-Oddr to Bjarmaland. The route followed is identical, and though Ohthere omits to tell us the *fela spella* related to him by the Bjarmar, he evidently heard and understood them ; and their suspicious character, which deterred him from relating them to the king, suggests that they may have been not wholly unlike those which we are gravely asked in the saga of Örvar-Oddr to believe happened before his eyes. Can it be that two men of the ruling class, both from Hálogaland, one called Óttarr, one Oddr, both great travellers, should make the same voyage from their home in the north of Norway up the northern Dvina about the same time, that both should be prevented by the hostility of the inhabitants from making a satisfactory landing, and that shortly afterwards both should find themselves at a king's court in England and on terms of friendship with him, recognising his superior power, and that at a time when the Norsemen and the English were in a deadly struggle with one another? These things are difficult to accept unless the two men were identical. It seems to me to be not impossible that in the account of the voyage of Ohthere we have an epitome of an Anglo-Saxon version of the early part of the voyage of Oddr the Far-travelled, even though the names are definitely not philologically related. Possibly the voyage of Wulfstan offers an epitome of some other Norse saga.

It is evident that about this time interest in Russia was very much to the fore. The burning question of the day was the exploitation of the Volga, the Kama, the Don, and the Dnêpr, and incidentally, as a means to this end, the northern and western Dvinas. It was this growing interest in Russia which made Oddr's journey to Bjarmaland so universally famous. Bjarmaland had sprung into fame, doubtless as the gate to the East. The explanation is probably to be sought in the recent Mohammedan conquests in the Mediterranean which had rendered hazardous the route through the Mediterranean to the East.

In these circumstances it is natural to suppose that the fame of pioneer exploration in Bjarmaland, whether round the North Cape or through the Baltic, would have more than a mere local interest. It would not be surprising if we should find the results recorded in more than one country, and in more than one form. It seems to me to be a probability—it can be no more than this—that the Norse hero Örvar-Oddr, of whom we have one of our fullest sagas, is the hero also of King Alfred's account of the voyage of Ohthere, and also of the earliest stories in the Russian Chronicle, themselves based on some form of saga. It is clear that each of these countries has preserved independently stories of a great pioneer in early Russian exploitation who lived in the latter part of the ninth century. We have seen also that while identical stories in some measure are told of the Norse and the Russian adventurers, the route of the first great voyage of the Norse traveller, Oddr Víthförli, 'The Far-travelled', is also identical with that of the Norse whale fisher of the English account. It is difficult to avoid at least a strong suspicion that we have before us three different versions of a single story.

It would not be difficult to see how the story of Oddr came to be remembered and recorded, whether in Scandinavia or in Russia. The evidence of his saga and of those of his father and his grandfather makes it clear that in the milieu in which the stories were recorded and transmitted, that is to say in Hálogaland, the cultivation of oral extempore poetry was exceptionally highly specialised. The sagas of Grímr Lothinkinni and Ketill Haengr in particular suggest that in this milieu, as on the steppes of

Central Asia down to the last century, formal conversation in polished circles was carried on almost wholly in poetical form. Both Ketill Haengr and Grímr Lothinkinni appear to have been expert in carrying on extempore poetical dialogue, and Oddr shows himself equally accomplished in this art, and also in more sustained compositions. We may refer, for example, to the fliting which he carries on at the ale feast at the court in Húnaland, where he arrives in disguise, and enters into poetical competition with Sigurthr and Sjólfr. We may refer again to another poem about his journey to Bjálkaland and to the death song which he is said to have composed while his funeral pyre was being constructed. Most of the longer poems in this saga are generally thought to have been composed by the compiler of the saga himself; but the persistence with which such poems are attributed in the saga to the leading characters, and the facility in poetical composition which is attributed to the family to which Oddr belonged, are surely significant. In view of the use which Snorri Sturluson and others, notably the anonymous compilers of the *Flateyjarbók*, make of poetry as a basis for their prose narratives, it is reasonable to suppose that the nucleus of this family history was derived from oral poems, traditionally ascribed to them. It has indeed been suggested that most of our knowledge of the Russia of the Viking Age is derived ultimately from the skalds who visited Russia, and it is very probable that our knowledge of Oddr the Far-travelled is derived from poems relating to his adventures abroad, and that some of these have gained currency in Russia and formed the basis of some of the early sagas incorporated in summary form in the *Povêst*.

It is interesting to reflect that all three of the enterprises which we have been examining—those of Oleg (Helgi), of Oddr, and of Ohthere—heading, as they were, for the great river systems of Russia, took place shortly before the great series of raids on the Caspian recorded by Oriental writers of the tenth and eleventh centuries. All this activity and enterprise, it is clear, can have had only one object, that of permanent expansion and settlement in the East analogous to those of the Norsemen in the West, with an ultimate design of trade and commercial development, involving as a necessary condition conquest and supremacy. Such a development was indeed a necessity if communications with the East were to be kept open for regular trade. The Mohammedan conquest had rendered the Mediterranean routes precarious, and the Pecheneg inroads had practically closed the southern steppes of Russia, while the conquest of the Frisians, the police of the seas, by Charlemagne, had rendered the North Sea equally unsafe for peaceful enterprise. But the Khazars on the Volga were open to terms with the 'Rus', and once communications had been established with them, e.g. up the northern Dvina and then down the Volga, the gate to the East lay open.

It is impossible to doubt that King Alfred was keenly aware of the movements and aspirations of the neighbouring peoples of Europe. However little credence one gives to William of Malmesbury's story of the mission to India made by the bishop of Sherborne in his reign, there can be no doubt that his little court of Wessex must have been one of the most cosmopolitan in Europe. Here were to be found John the Old Saxon, Grimbald from Flanders, Plegmund the Mercian, Asser the Welshman. There were Frisians in his fleet. Irish anchorites made their way to his court, and there is other evidence to show that he was intimately aware of events happening in Ireland. He was in touch with Gaul. Despite his constant struggle for existence in an enemy-occupied country, his court was a centre of culture and book learning, a little sub-classical world. And here Ohthere the whaler came from the north of Norway 'to his lord King Alfred' to report on his unsuccessful attempt to make a north-east passage to the Orient. The attempt is carefully registered, alongside other information bearing on the same subject. We cannot doubt that Ohthere had every reason to know that his information had more than a mere academic interest for the English court, and that the burning question of the moment, here, as elsewhere, was how best to pick up the strands of intercourse with the wealthy Orient, which had been broken since the downfall of the Sassanian Empire.

INDEX

Agriculture, 16, 112, 118, 119, 127 (ploughing)
Alani, 43
Alexander the Great, Persian romance of, 58–9
Alfred the Great, 21, Appendix II
Altun Apa, 128
Andrew, king of Hungary, 109
Andrey, son of Vladimir II, 123
Anna, Greek princess, married to Vladimir I, 71, 106
Arabic records, etc., ix, 50, 52, 72, 74
Arabs, 46, 69
Askold, 15, 20, 22
Ásmundr (Asmund), 27, 28, 116
Avars, 17
Ay Apa, 128
Azarbaijan, 51, 52
Azov, Sea of, 14, 43

Baghdad, 14, 70
Bandyuk (Ban Dyuk), 125
Banner, 92, 93
Barda'a, raid on, 51, 52, 54–6, 57–60, Appendix I
Barrows, 26, 29, 81, 87, 94
Basil II, Greek Emperor, 72
Bath house, 30
Beldyuz, 128
Bêlo-ozero, 19, 119
Berestovoye, 126
Bjarmaland, Temple of, 90
Björn Hítdoelakappi, 65
Black Sea, 14, 27, 69
Blud, 9, 36, 37, 67, 81, 113
Boleslav of Poland, 99, 100, 103, 113, 127
Bonyak, 126, 127, 128

Books in a cave, 46
Boris (brother of Svyatopolk), 98, 121
Boyars, 20, 65, 95, 99, 129
Brest in Lithuania, 100, 103
Budy, 99, 114, 116
Bulan, prince of the Khazars, 43
Bulgars, Bulgarians, 14, 17, 32, 33, 43, 45, 68, 69, 70, 103, 118
Burial, 53
ship, 29, 30, 54, 81
Byzantium, 9, 10, 20, 22, 23, 27, 30, 31, 33, 43, 44, 48, 70, 71, 75, 105, 108, 111, 114, 129, 131, 134

'Cambridge Document', 41, 43
Caspian, Russian invasions into, 50–61
Caspian Sea, 14, 50, 51
Catholics, 69
Cave churches, 46, 69
Chernigov, 22, 103, 107, 123
Christianity, 23, 31, 62, 68, 70, 71, 76, 98
Church, Greek, 31, 76, 121, 136
Russian, 3, 8, 35, 108, 110, 130, 131
of St Michael of the Gilded Dome, 129
Constantine V (Greek Emperor), 14
Constantine Kosnyachek, 121
Constantine, son of Dobrynya, 67, 99, 113, 114
Constantinople, see Byzantium
Crimea, 43, 45, 68 (note) 1), 96, 129
Cumani, see Polovtsy